# FREE WILL

**The MIT Press Essential Knowledge Series**

# FREE WILL

## MARK BALAGUER

The MIT Press | Cambridge, Massachusetts | London, England

This book was set in Chaparral Pro by the MIT Press. Printed and bound in the United States of America.

Library of Congress Cataloging-in-Publication Data

Balaguer, Mark.
Free will / Mark Balaguer.
    pages    cm.—(The MIT Press essential knowledge series)
Includes bibliographical references and index.
ISBN 978-0-262-52579-4 (pbk. : alk. paper)
1. Free will and determinism.  I. Title.
BJ1460.B35    2014
123'.5—dc23

                                                        2013028479

10   9   8   7   6   5

This book is dedicated to Ellen Balaguer and Paul Balaguer, my sister and brother, for always being there for me since before I can remember.

# CONTENTS

# SERIES FOREWORD

The MIT Press Essential Knowledge series offers accessible, concise, beautifully produced pocket-size books on topics of current interest. Written by leading thinkers, the books in this series deliver expert overviews of subjects that range from the cultural and the historical to the scientific and the technical.

In today's era of instant information gratification, we have ready access to opinions, rationalizations, and superficial descriptions. Much harder to come by is the foundational knowledge that informs a principled understanding of the world. Essential Knowledge books fill that need. Synthesizing specialized subject matter for nonspecialists and engaging critical topics through fundamentals, each of these compact volumes offers readers a point of access to complex ideas.

*Bruce Tidor*
*Professor of Biological Engineering and Computer Science*
*Massachusetts Institute of Technology*

# ACKNOWLEDGMENTS

I would like to thank the following people (mostly family members) for offering helpful feedback on earlier drafts of this book: Ellen Balaguer, Marcella Balaguer, Melchor Balaguer, Paul Balaguer, Judy Feldmann, Michael McKenna, and two anonymous referees.

# INTRODUCTION

In the last few years, several people have argued that science has shown us that human beings don't have free will. People like Daniel Wegner (a Harvard psychologist) and Sam Harris (a neuroscientist and the author of various "popular philosophy" books) claim that certain scientific findings reveal that free will is an *illusion*.

If this were true, it would be less than splendid. And it would be surprising, too, because it really *seems* like we have free will. It seems that what we do from moment to moment is determined by conscious decisions that we freely make. Suppose, for instance, that I'm lying on my couch watching TV, and I suddenly decide to get up and go for a walk. It seems that the *reason* that I got up and went for a walk is that I made a conscious *decision* to do so. I could have kept watching TV, or I could have done something completely different. Hell, I could have painted myself green and pretended I was the Incredible Hulk, engaged in a battle to the death with an evil troupe of Lithuanian trapeze artists. But I didn't; I went for a walk. And when I did that, I exercised my free will. Or so it seems to us. But if people like Wegner and Harris are right, then this feeling of freedom that we all have is an illusion. On their view, we don't really have free will. In other words, we don't have any real choice about what we do. Rather, on their view, everything we do is completely caused by things that are totally out of our control. And, again, according to these people, there is *scientific evidence* that supports the claim that we don't have free will.

I don't trust these people. It's not that I don't trust *science*. On the contrary, I *really* trust science. I think it's the best way we have of acquiring knowledge about the world. I just don't trust *people*. And I really don't trust people who tell me that science has shown that some crazy claim is true. Now, don't get me wrong—I'm fully aware that science has already shown us that lots of crazy claims are true. But for every case where science has legitimately established the truth of some crazy-sounding result, there are a thousand cases where people erroneously claim that science has established a crazy-sounding result. So the moral here is this: Just because someone with a PhD and a lab coat tells you that science has established some nutty conclusion doesn't mean it's really true. Of course, it doesn't mean it's *false* either. My claim is simply that we have to check it out for ourselves.

So I'm completely open to the idea that science could establish that we don't have free will. After all, our decision-making processes are brain processes. In particular, they're neural processes, and neural processes are obviously in the domain of scientific investigation. That's just what neuroscience does—it studies neural processes. So it's a real possibility that neuroscientists could discover that we don't have free will. I'm just not sure that they *have* discovered this. So I want to look for myself and see if they're right.

That's what this book is going to be about. I'm going to discuss and evaluate the various arguments and scientific experiments that people have put forward in support of the claim that human beings don't have free will. By the end of the book, we'll be able to answer the question of whether the various arguments are any good; in other words, we'll be able to say whether we really do have good reason to give up our belief in free will.

Before going any further, I want to bring out an issue that will be relevant to our discussion. Broadly speaking, we can endorse two different views about the nature of human beings. These two views can be summarized as follows:

> *The spiritual, religious view of humans* Every person has an immortal *soul*, or a nonphysical *spirit*, that's distinct from the physical body and that somehow

It's a real possibility that neuroscientists could discover that we don't have free will. I'm just not sure that they *have* discovered this.

"drives" the body, or "tells the body what to do." For instance, if you're thirsty and you consciously decide to go into the kitchen to get a glass of water, then it's your soul that makes this conscious decision and causes your body to get up and start walking.

*The materialistic, scientific view of humans*    There is no more to a human being than his or her physical body. There is no nonphysical soul in addition to the body. So everything about you that makes you who you are can be found in your brain. Your beliefs and desires, your hopes and fears, your memories, your feelings of love and hate—these are all in your brain, coded by neural pathways. And if we want to know why you got up and walked into the kitchen, we just have to look at your brain. There's nowhere else to look, because you don't have a nonphysical soul. Your thirstiness was a physical thing, neurally coded in your brain. Moreover, your conscious decision to go get some water was *also* physical—it was a physical, neural event that occurred in your brain. And this neural event caused your muscles to move, and so on and so forth.

The debate between these two views is obviously very heated and controversial in its own right, and I am not going to try to settle this debate here. But the difference between these two views of human beings is important to our topic for a few reasons. The first point to note is that the scientific enemies of free will—people like Wegner and Harris, who think that science has shown that we don't have free will—generally assume something like a materialistic, scientific view of humans.

Now, given this, you might think, "So, if I believe in God, and if I believe that I have a nonphysical soul, then I don't have to worry about the arguments that these people have given. I don't have to worry that I might not have free will."

But it's not obvious that this is right. It may be that the belief in souls doesn't solve the problem. In other words, it may be that even if you accept the spiritual, religious view—even if you believe that we all possess nonphysical souls that drive our bodies—you can't use this belief to weasel out of the arguments against free will. It may be that the arguments against free will still go through. We'll have to see about this.

In any event, whatever we say about whether the spiritual, religious view can be used to block the arguments against free will, I'm going to spend much more time looking for a response to the anti-free-will arguments that we can *all* use, regardless of whether we believe in nonphysical souls. In doing this, I will often be assuming for the sake of argument that the materialistic, scientific view of humans is correct. In other words, the question I'll be trying to answer is whether we can find a way of responding to the arguments against free will *if we assume that human beings don't have nonphysical souls*. My idea here is that if we can find a way for *materialists* to respond to the anti-free-will arguments, then advocates of the spiritual, religious view should be able to respond in a similar way. So by proceeding in this fashion, we'll actually be looking for a response that everyone can use.

But in the spirit of disclosure—so you know who you're listening to here—let me lay my cards on the table. I don't believe in God, and I don't believe in nonphysical souls. I'm not a mad-dog, foaming-at-the-mouth atheist, but I just in fact don't believe that there are any such things as Gods or nonphysical souls. But this view of mine won't really matter in this book because, again, I'm going to be looking for an answer to the arguments against free will that we can *all* use, and what's more, I'm going to address the question of whether we can escape the anti-free-will arguments by abandoning materialism and endorsing the idea that we all have nonphysical souls.

Before getting down to business, I should probably say something about the fact that free will is *important* to us. This is a point that's often made by people writing on this topic. They tell us that free will is central to morality, religion, politics, and our legal system. Indeed, we're told that free will is crucial to our conception of ourselves as human beings.

This is perhaps all true, but I smell a rat. This sounds to me like an attempt to justify the decision to write about free will. Moreover, I think that these high-brow, noble-sounding musings fail to get at the *main* reason that we care about the question of whether we have free will. The main reason we care about this question is that we *want* free will. We want it for the same reason that we want ice cream and happiness and sex—because it's *good*. Free will is just an intrinsically good thing that we all want. So if it turned out that we don't have it—that the feeling of free will is an illusion—that would just be *bad*.

But, of course, even if free will is intrinsically desirable, it might also be true that it's important as a means to other things. For instance, you might think that we need free will in order to justify the way that we treat criminals. You might think that if people don't have free will, then no one deserves to be punished. Consider, for instance, Bruno Hauptmann, who was convicted of kidnapping and murdering Charles Lindbergh's baby. Most people would say that if Hauptmann was in fact guilty, then he deserved to be punished for his crimes. But if he didn't have any free will—if his actions were caused by things that were completely out of his control, so that he didn't have any genuine choice about what he did—then it's hard to see how his actions were his fault, and it's hard to see how it could be fair to blame him. We might still incarcerate criminals like this—just to protect ourselves—but if they don't have free will, then it's hard to see how they *deserve* this treatment.

The moral thinking behind this argument might be right, but I have a hard time believing that there's anything of real pragmatic use here. Even if we became utterly convinced that people don't have free will, nothing much would change. It would be big news for a few days, but then we'd get bored and move on to the next big thing—like Lindsay Lohan getting a DUI, or whatever. And if after the discovery that humans don't have free will, someone kidnapped and murdered your baby, I'm betting dollars to donuts that you'd feel moral outrage; you'd feel in your heart that the murderer *deserved* to be punished, free will or no free will.

People are people, and if we really discovered that we don't have free will, I don't think it would change much of anything. But this doesn't mean that it wouldn't be big news. It would. And it would be *bad* news. It would be like learning that there was no more chocolate. It wouldn't be the end of the world if we found out that we would have to make do without chocolate, and within a few days, we'd move on; we'd start eating more vanilla and caramel, and that would be the end of it. But this doesn't change the fact that we *like* chocolate and we don't want to live without it. And the same goes for free will.

(An anonymous referee for this book objected here on the grounds that some people *don't* like chocolate. If this were true, it would of course be devastating to my argument, but I don't believe it for a second. Most people who claim not to like chocolate are dirty liars who can usually be discovered sneaking Snickers bars behind the dumpster in the parking lot, and the remaining few who honestly believe that they don't like chocolate are simply confused. They usually just haven't tried chocolate in the right setting. If you're in this category, try eating an entire Sara Lee chocolate cake while lying in bed, under the covers, with the curtains drawn, watching reruns of *As the World Turns*. I think you'll be surprised at the results.)

# THE CASE AGAINST FREE WILL

I want to start by presenting the arguments against free will. Later, I'll try to figure out whether these arguments are any good, but in this chapter, I just want to formulate the arguments in the strongest way I can, as the enemies of free will conceive of them.

The central idea behind the arguments against free will is the idea of *determinism*, so I'll begin there.

### Determinism

Let's start off by thinking about pool balls. Suppose you hit a cue ball into an eight ball, and the eight ball goes into a corner pocket. Given the way that the cue ball hit the eight ball—given the exact force of the impact, and the exact way that the cue ball was spinning, and so on—it seems that there was only one thing that the eight ball could have done.

In other words, it seems that the way that the cue ball hit the eight ball *determined* the path that the eight ball would follow. It seems that the eight ball couldn't have done anything else. You can think of this in terms of the laws of physics. It seems that the eight ball was *forced* to behave in the way that it did by the laws of physics, or the laws of nature.

Determinism is the view that *all* events are like this. It's the view that every physical event is *completely caused* by prior events together with the laws of nature. Or, to put the point differently, it's the view that every event has a cause that *makes* it happen in the one and only way that it could have happened.

(Actually, this characterization of determinism is a bit rough. If you want a precise definition, we can say that determinism is the view that a complete statement of the laws of nature, together with a complete description of the universe at some specific time, logically entails a complete description of the universe at all later times.)

But however we define determinism, the main point I want to make here is that, intuitively, it seems right. Indeed, it can seem downright obvious. To see why, consider a different case involving pool balls. Suppose that we set up two balls right next to each other and that you and I hit them simultaneously, very lightly, with our pool cues. And suppose that my ball rolls 12 inches before stopping, whereas your ball rolls 12.1 inches. Given this, let's ask the following question: why did your ball go farther than mine did?

Well, the obvious answer is that you hit your ball a bit harder than I did. But, of course, there are other possible explanations we might give. It could be that we hit the balls with equal force but that your ball weighs a bit less than mine. Or it could be that there was a bit more friction on the part of the table that my ball rolled over. Or whatever. We might not know the answer to the above question, but it seems clear that there has to *be* an answer. But imagine someone responding to our question by saying this:

> There's no reason why your ball went farther. It just *did*. The two balls have the exact same mass; and they were hit with the exact same force; and there were exactly equivalent amounts of friction on the two parts of the table; and so on. In short, there were *no* differences between the two cases. The one ball just went farther than the other one did, and that's all there is to it. In other words, nothing caused this to happen; it just *did*.

Intuitively, this seems crazy. It would seem very natural to respond to this little speech by saying something like the following:

> What in the Sam Hill are you talking about? Physical events don't just *happen*. If one ball went farther than

the other one did, then there has to be a *reason* for this. Something must have *caused* it to go farther.

This *seems* right. But notice that this is just what a determinist would say. To say that things don't just happen is essentially equivalent to saying that every event is completely caused by prior events.

So, again, determinism seems very plausible. But it's also important to note that determinism has some very striking consequences. Notice, for instance, that if determinism is true, then as soon as the Big Bang took place 13 billion years ago, the entire history of the universe was already settled. In other words, it was already determined that everything would take place exactly as it *has* taken place. It was already determined, for instance, that there would be a tsunami in Japan in 2011. Why? Because if determinism is true, then every time something happens, there's only *one* next thing that can happen. So once the Big Bang happened, the next event was *forced on us* by the laws of physics; and then the next event after that was forced on us as well; and likewise for the next one, and the next one, and the next one, all the way through history. So according to determinism, once the Big Bang happened, it was just an inevitable step-by-step 13-billion-year march to the 2011 tsunami. That's a pretty striking claim.

## The Classical Argument Against Free Will

There's a very old argument against free will that's based on the assumption that determinism is true. If determinism is true, then it was already settled 13 billion years ago, right after the Big Bang occurred, that there would be a tsunami in Japan in 2011. But that's not all. The point applies to *us* as well. For instance, it was also already settled that in that same infamous year—indeed, within weeks of the tsunami—Charlie Sheen was going to go on national TV and proclaim not just that he was a warlock but that he had "Adonis DNA" (a term I'm assuming he got from biologists). Or to strike a bit closer to home, it was already settled that you would be reading this book right now. In fact, if determinism is true, then everything you've ever done—every choice you've ever made—was already determined 13 billion years ago. But if this is true, then it has obvious implications for free will.

Suppose that you're in an ice cream parlor, waiting in line, trying to decide whether to order chocolate or vanilla ice cream. And suppose that when you get to the front of the line, you decide to order chocolate. Was this choice a product of your free will? Well, if determinism is true, then your choice was completely caused by prior events. The *immediate* causes of the decision were neural events that occurred in your brain just prior to your choice. But,

If determinism is true, then everything you've ever done—every choice you've ever made—was already determined 13 billion years ago.

of course, if determinism is true, then those neural events that caused your decision had physical causes as well; they were caused by even earlier events—events that occurred just before they did. And so on, stretching back into the past. We can follow this back to when you were a baby, to the very first events of your life. In fact, we can keep going back before that, because if determinism is true, then those first events were also caused by prior events. We can keep going back to events that occurred before you were even conceived, to events involving your mother and father and a bottle of Chianti.

So if determinism is true, then it was already settled before you were born that you were going to order chocolate ice cream when you got to the front of the line. But if this is true, then it would seem to follow that you didn't order chocolate ice cream of your own free will. And, of course, the same can be said about *all* of our decisions. If determinism is true, then every choice that any human being has ever made was already predetermined by events that took place billions of years ago, before our solar system even existed. And so it seems that if determinism is true, then human beings do not have free will.

Let's call this the *classical argument against free will*. It proceeds by assuming that determinism is true and arguing from there that we don't have free will.

## Is Determinism Really True?

There's a big problem with the classical argument against free will. It just *assumes* that determinism is true. The idea behind the argument seems to be that determinism is just a commonsense truism. But it's actually not a commonsense truism. Now, I said a few paragraphs back that, *intuitively*, determinism seems right. But one of the main lessons of twentieth-century physics is that we can't know by common sense, or by intuition, that determinism is true. Determinism is a controversial hypothesis about the workings of the physical world. We could only know that it's true by doing some high-level physics. Moreover—and this is another lesson of twentieth-century physics—as of right now, we don't have any good *evidence* for determinism. In other words, our best physical theories don't answer the question of whether determinism is true.

During the reign of classical physics (or Newtonian physics), it was widely believed that determinism was true. But in the late nineteenth and early twentieth centuries, physicists started to discover some problems with Newton's theory, and it was eventually replaced with a new theory—*quantum mechanics*. (Actually, it was replaced by two new theories, namely, quantum mechanics and relativity theory. But relativity theory isn't relevant to the topic of free will.) Quantum mechanics has several strange and interesting features, but the one that's relevant to free will is that this new theory contains laws that are *probabilistic* rather than deterministic. We can understand what this means very easily. Roughly speaking, deterministic laws of nature look like this:

If you have a physical system in state S, and if you perform experiment E on that system, then you will get outcome O.

But quantum physics contains probabilistic laws that look like this:

If you have a physical system in state S, and if you perform experiment E on that system, then there are two different possible outcomes, namely, O1 and O2; moreover, there's a 50 percent chance that you'll get outcome O1 and a 50 percent chance that you'll get outcome O2.

It's important to notice what follows from this. Suppose that we take a physical system, put it into state S, and perform experiment E on it. Now suppose that when we perform this experiment, we get outcome O1. Finally, suppose we ask the following question: "Why did we get outcome O1 instead of O2?" The important point to notice is that *quantum mechanics doesn't answer this question*. It doesn't give us any explanation at all for why we got outcome O1 instead of O2. In other words, as far as quantum mechanics is concerned, it could be that *nothing caused us to get result O1*; it could be that this just *happened*.

Now, Einstein famously thought that this couldn't be the whole story. You've probably heard that he once said that "God doesn't play dice with the universe." What he meant when he said this was that the fundamental laws of nature can't be probabilistic. The fundamental laws, Einstein thought, have to tell us what *will* happen next, not what will *probably* happen, or what *might* happen. So Einstein thought that there had to be a *hidden layer of reality*, below the quantum level, and that if we could find this hidden layer, we could get rid of the probabilistic laws of quantum mechanics and replace them with *deterministic* laws, laws that tell us what *will* happen next, not just what will *probably* happen next. And, of course, if we could do this—if we could find this hidden layer of reality and these deterministic laws of nature—then we would be able to explain why we got outcome O1 instead of O2.

But a lot of other physicists—most notably, Werner Heisenberg and Niels Bohr—disagreed with Einstein. They thought that the quantum layer of reality was the *bottom* layer. And they thought that the fundamental laws of nature—or at any rate, *some* of these laws—were probabilistic laws. But if this is right, then it means that at least some physical events aren't deterministically caused by prior events. It means that some physical events *just happen*. For instance, if Heisenberg and Bohr are right, then nothing caused us to get outcome O1 instead of O2; there was no *reason* why this happened; it just *did*.

The debate between Einstein on the one hand and Heisenberg and Bohr on the other is crucially important to our discussion. Einstein is a determinist. If he's right, then every physical event is predetermined—or in other words, completely caused by prior events. But if Heisenberg and Bohr are right, then determinism is *false*. On their view, not every event is predetermined by the past and the laws of nature; some things just *happen*, for no reason at all. In other words, if Heisenberg and Bohr are right, then *indeterminism* is true.

And here's the really important point for us. The debate between determinists like Einstein and indeterminists like Heisenberg and Bohr has never been settled. We don't have any good evidence for either view. Quantum mechanics is still our best theory of the subatomic world, but we just don't know whether there's another layer of reality, beneath the quantum layer. And so we don't know whether all physical events are completely caused by prior events. In other words, we don't know whether determinism or indeterminism is true. Future physicists might be able to settle this question, but as of right now, we don't know the answer.

But now notice that if we don't know whether determinism is true or false, then this completely undermines the classical argument against free will. That argument just assumed that determinism is true. But we now know that there is no good reason to believe this. The question of whether determinism is true is an open question for physicists. So the classical argument against free will is a failure—it doesn't give us any good reason to conclude that we don't have free will.

## The New-and-Improved Arguments Against Free Will

We just found that the classical argument against free will doesn't work. But the enemies of free will are completely undeterred by this. They still think there's a powerful argument to be made against free will. In fact, they think there are *two* such arguments. Both of these arguments can be thought of as attempts to fix the classical argument, but as we will see, they do this in completely different ways.

### The First Argument Against Free Will: The Random-Or-Predetermined Argument

The first argument against free will is based on the idea that even if determinism isn't true, we still don't have free will. To see why a lot of people believe this, let's go back to your decision to order chocolate ice cream. There are two different possibilities here:

1. Your choice was caused by prior events.

2. Your choice wasn't caused by prior events.

The problem is that it seems that *both* of these possibilities are incompatible with the idea that you chose of your own free will. Now, we've already argued that the first possibility is incompatible with free will, because this is just the case where your choice was completely predetermined by the past. What we need to think about, then, is the second case—the case where your choice *wasn't* caused by prior events. In this case, your decision was still a neural event that occurred in your brain, but now we're supposed to imagine that nothing caused it to occur. Nothing *made* it happen. In other words, it just *happened*. The neurons could have fired in a different way—they could have fired in a way that made you order vanilla—but, in fact, they didn't. They fired in a way that made you order chocolate.

But wait. To say that your decision *just happened* is just to say that it happened *randomly*. But if your decision occurred randomly, then that's no more compatible with free will than if it was causally predetermined by prior events. Think about it for a minute. If your decision just randomly appeared in your brain, then how could it be right to say that you chose of your own free will? That wouldn't make any sense at all. To say that you chose of your own free will is to say that you were responsible for the choice, and that you were in control of the choice. But none of this is true if the decision just randomly appeared in your brain. Therefore, it seems clear that if our decisions occur randomly—if they just randomly appear in our brains—then we do not have free will.

This gives rise to a powerful argument against free will. There are only two possibilities here—our decisions are either caused by prior events or not caused by prior events—and *both* of these possibilities rule out free will. If our decisions *are* caused by prior events, then they're not the products of our free will because they're predetermined by the past. And if they're *not* caused by prior events, then they're not the products of our free will because they just *happen*—because they just randomly appear in our brains. So either way, we don't have free will.

So that's the first argument against free will. Let's call it the *random-or-predetermined argument*. It's an extremely powerful argument; it's much more formidable than the classical argument, and in recent years it has become much more popular, especially among professional philosophers.

Before moving on to the second argument against free will, I want to make two quick points about the random-or-predetermined argument. First, the conclusion of this argument isn't just that we don't *have* free will. It's that free will is *impossible*. Indeed, if the random-or-predetermined argument is right, then the whole idea of free will is *incoherent*. For a decision to be truly free, it has to satisfy two different conditions:

(i) It can't be predetermined by prior events.

(ii) It can't be random.

But the whole point of the random-or-predetermined argument is that it's literally *impossible* to satisfy both of these requirements at the same time. The idea is that if our decisions *are* caused then they don't satisfy condition (i), and if they're *not* caused then they don't satisfy condition (ii).

The second point I want to make about the random-or-predetermined argument is that I have simplified it a bit. If you're curious about this, you can read this section, and I will explain how I've simplified it and what the unsimplified version of the argument looks like. I want to warn you in advance, however, that this section is a bit nitpicky, and what's more, it's not really necessary for the rest of the book. So if you're not in a nitpicky mood, you can skip down to the next section and read on from there. You won't have missed anything that will matter to the rest of the book.

The first thing we need to do, to understand the simplification, is to distinguish two different kinds of causation—*deterministic* causation and *probabilistic* causation. We can define these two kinds of causation as follows:

A. To say that an event was *deterministically* caused by prior events is to say that it was *completely* caused by prior events. In other words, it's to say that it was *completely predetermined*, so that prior events *forced* it to happen in the one and only way that it could have happened.

B. To say that an event was *probabilistically* caused, on the other hand, is to say that it was caused by prior events but that these prior events didn't *force* it to happen. Rather, the prior events simply *increased the probability* that the event in question would happen.

Given this, it seems that, strictly speaking, when the enemies of free will articulate the random-or-predetermined argument against free will, they need to distinguish *three* possibilities, not two. For any given decision, the three possibilities are as follows:

1. The decision is completely caused (or deterministically caused) by prior events.

2. The decision is completely uncaused.

3. The decision is probabilistically caused (but not deterministically caused) by prior events.

As I've set things up here, the random-or-predetermined argument consists in arguing that the first two possibilities are incompatible with free will. Therefore, strictly speaking, the authors of this argument need to argue that the third possibility is *also* incompatible with free will. But it turns out that this isn't very hard to do. The enemies of free will can do it by saying something like this:

If a decision is probabilistically caused but not deterministically caused, then it's partially caused and partially uncaused. But insofar as it's caused, it's not free because it's predetermined; and insofar as it's uncaused, it's not free because it's random. So the third possibility is no more compatible with free will than the first two, because it's really just a mixture of the first two.

So the difference between the simplified and unsimplified versions of the random-or-predetermined argument is that the latter includes a discussion of the third possibility. But this doesn't really change things very much. It doesn't change the *feel* of the random-or-predetermined argument, and more importantly for us, it won't change things when we go to *evaluate* the argument. So just to make things easy, I'm going to ignore this complication; in other words, in what follows, when I talk about the random-or-predetermined argument, I will be talking about the *simplified* version—the one that focuses on the first two possibilities and ignores the third.

### The Second Argument Against Free Will: The Scientific Argument

The second argument against free will is based on the following claim:

> There is strong empirical evidence for the idea that our actions and decisions are completely caused by nonconscious events that we have no control over.

The earliest evidence for this came from psychologists, who discovered that many of our actions and decisions are caused by things that we're completely unaware of. We have known for a long time, for instance, that our behavior can be influenced by things like subliminal messages. Moreover, when our behavior is influenced by things like this, we construct elaborate stories (or as psychologists say, we *confabulate* stories) to explain why we did what we did. We *think* these explanations are true, but they aren't; they're completely false. In short, psychologists have produced ample evidence for the claim that we are often totally mistaken about why we do what we do.

We've all heard the stories of these studies. If the owner of a movie theater splices a single frame of a bag of popcorn into the middle of a movie, people in the theater won't consciously notice it at all, but they will be much more likely to get up and go buy popcorn. These studies can be pretty depressing. They can make you embarrassed to be human. (And to be honest, the whole thing makes me a bit nervous about going to the movies. I mean, God knows what kinds of weird things they could get me to do. I can just hear the puzzled questions I'd get later from my wife: "Honey? ... I just got off the phone with Mrs. Kravitz. Did you sneak into their house and put my eczema cream in their freezer?")

In any event, to return to the discussion of the scientific argument against free will, the most compelling evidence here comes not from psychologists but from neuroscientists. These people have discovered some neural events that occur in our heads—some purely physical, nonconscious *brain* events—that occur *before* we make our conscious decisions and that seem to determine how these decisions will go. In other words, the neural events in question seem to be the physical causes of our decisions.

Several neuroscientific experiments are relevant here, but the first of these experiments, and the most famous of them, were performed by Benjamin Libet in 1983. Libet was building on a previous neuroscientific discovery from the 1960s. It was discovered then that conscious decisions are associated with a certain kind of brain activity known as the *readiness potential*. (It doesn't really matter what the readiness potential is, but for the curious, it's a shift in electrical potential that's measurable on the scalp.) In Libet's study, subjects sat facing a large, specially designed clock that could measure time in milliseconds. Subjects were told to flick their wrists whenever they felt an urge to do so and to note the exact time that they felt the conscious urge to move. Meanwhile, Libet used EEG to measure the subjects' brains. He found that the readiness potential—the physical brain activity associated with our decisions—arose about a half a second *before* the conscious intention to move.

These studies became immediately famous, and they have been enormously influential. The reason they're so important is that many people think they deliver a death blow to free will. The argument here is simple. It can be put like this:

When you perform an action, if you don't make a conscious decision to act until *after* the physical causes of your action have already been set in motion, then the idea that you have free will is an illusion. It simply makes no sense to say that you decided to flick your wrist of your own free will if the physical causes of your action were already in motion before you made your conscious choice.

In the thirty years since Libet first published his results, numerous scientists have performed similar experiments. People have changed various things about the experimental setup, and they have produced some very interesting results. But the most striking follow-up studies have been performed very recently by J. D. Haynes. Haynes's subjects were given two buttons, one for their left hand and one for their right hand, and they were told to make a decision at some point as to whether to press the left button or the right button and to go ahead and push the given button as soon as they made their decision. Using fMRI instead of EEG, Haynes found unconscious brain activity that predicted whether subjects would press the left button or the right; and he found that this activity arose *seven to ten seconds before* the person made a conscious decision to push the given button.

This is pretty stunning. If you're about to choose between two options, and if somebody watching your brain could predict which of the two options you're going to choose *a full seven seconds before you make your conscious choice*, then clearly, the conscious choosing isn't responsible for determining what you do. What you were going to do was already settled before you made the decision. And if that's right, then it's hard to see how it makes any sense at all to say that you have free will.

**The Two Arguments in a Nutshell**

To sum things up, there are two different arguments for the conclusion that we don't have free will. They can be put like this:

> *The random-or-predetermined argument against free will*   Our decisions are either caused by prior events or *not* caused by prior events. If they *are* caused by prior events, then they're not the products of our free will because they're predetermined by prior events. And if they're *not* caused by prior events, then they're not the products of our free will because they happen *randomly,* and it makes no sense to say that we have free will if our choices just randomly appear in our brains.

> *The scientific argument against free will*   There is strong scientific evidence (from psychology and neuroscience) that supports the claim that our conscious decisions are completely caused by events that occur *before* we choose, that are completely out of our control, and indeed, that we're completely unaware of.

It's worth noting that both of these arguments can be seen as attempts to fix the classical argument against free will. The classical argument proceeded by assuming that determinism is true and arguing that this rules out free will. The problem with this argument is that we don't have any good reason to think that determinism is really true. But given this, we can think of advocates of the random-or-predetermined argument as responding to the situation by saying this:

It doesn't matter whether determinism is true, because indeterminism is just as incompatible with free will as determinism is.

And we can think of advocates of the scientific argument as responding to the situation by saying this:

It doesn't matter whether the full-blown hypothesis of determinism is true, because it doesn't matter whether *all* events are predetermined by prior events. All that matters is whether *our decisions* are predetermined by prior events. And the point of the scientific argument against free will is that we have good evidence for thinking that they *are*.

Finally, it's important to note that whereas the scientific argument is (obviously) a *scientific* argument, the random-or-predetermined argument is *not* a scientific argument. It doesn't rely on any scientific evidence. It's a *philosophical* argument.

# CAN RELIGION SAVE FREE WILL?

It might seem that we could respond to the arguments against free will by adopting the spiritual, religious view of humans. In particular, you might think we could respond by saying something like this:

> *Spiritual-religious response to the anti-free-will arguments*   The arguments against free will that were described in chapter 2 seem to assume that human beings are purely physical things, made up of nothing but physical particles that move around according to the laws of physics. Well, if you have *that* view of human beings, it's no wonder there's no room for free will. But there's another view of human beings, namely, the spiritual, religious view, which holds that each of us possesses a nonphysical soul that's distinct from the physical body. If this is right, then human beings aren't subject to the laws

of physics in the way that pool balls are. A conscious human decision is fundamentally different from a pool shot. A pool shot is a purely physical event. But a conscious decision isn't purely physical. It's something that a person *does*. It's an act that's performed by a nonphysical soul. And so it's not governed by the laws of physics.

I want to say two things in response to this little speech, one very quick, and the other a bit longer. The quick point is just this: even if it's true that we can avoid the arguments against free will by embracing the spiritual, religious view of humans, this will only be a plausible response for *part* of the population, because there are a lot of people out there (me included) who don't believe the spiritual, religious view. So for these people, the question remains whether there's some other way of avoiding the arguments against free will.

The second, longer point I want to make here is that I don't think the spiritual-religious response to the anti-free-will arguments *works*. In other words, even if it's true that each of us possesses a nonphysical soul, I don't think we can use this to block the arguments against free will. We can understand why this is so by running through the two arguments against free will and seeing how they still stand, even if we assume that people have nonphysical souls. I will do this in a moment. But first I want to make a preliminary point. I want to explain why it can still make perfect sense to say that our decisions are *caused*, even if we endorse the spiritual, religious view of humans.

## The Causation of Decisions and the Spiritual, Religious View of Humans

Even if the spiritual, religious view of humans is right, we still might want to say that our decisions and actions can be *caused*. To appreciate this, consider the following story:

> Tracy wants to go home to visit her mother. She knows she can go either by plane or by train. But Tracy has an intense, irrational fear of flying; every time she thinks about it, she has vivid images of her plane falling out of the sky like a bag of dirt and exploding on impact; she sees herself clear as day, being thrown from the fiery wreckage and impaled on a stalk of corn in the middle of a farm in Iowa. On the other hand, Tracy absolutely *loves* trains; she has romantic ideas about seeing the heartland of America through the window of a dining car and weird fantasies that take place in boiler rooms with men wearing engineer's caps. (She is unaware that boiler rooms are actually on ships, not trains, and her analyst doesn't want to disabuse her of this delusion

for fear that it may trigger an "episode.") Finally, Tracy believes that a train ticket will be less expensive than a plane ticket. She is aware that it will take a bit longer to travel by train—in particular, it will take twelve hours instead of two—but Tracy doesn't mind this. In fact, she likes the idea. She has a desire to relax on the train for a day before seeing her mother, who can be ... well, let's just say she can be *difficult*, and leave it at that. So Tracy decides to buy a train ticket instead of a plane ticket.

Now, let's ask whether Tracy's decision to buy a train ticket was caused by anything. The obvious answer is that it *was*. It was caused by her *love* of trains, and her *fear* of flying, and her *belief* that a train ticket would be less expensive, and her *desire* to spend a day on the train before seeing her mother. In short, it seems that Tracy's decision was caused by her beliefs and desires and fears and so on. And here's the really important point for us: this seems to be true regardless of whether we believe in nonphysical souls. Now, the point that I ultimately want to make here is that advocates of the *spiritual*, *religious* view can say that Tracy's decision was caused by her beliefs and desires and so on. But first let me pause for a minute to make sure it's clear that advocates of the *materialistic*, *scientific* view can say that Tracy's decision was caused by these things. It might seem that they *can't* say this; it might seem that advocates of the materialistic, scientific view have to say this instead:

Our decisions are *physical* events. In particular, they're neural events. So if our decisions are caused at all, they have to be caused by other physical events, not things like beliefs and desires and fears.

This is an utter confusion. Advocates of the materialistic, scientific view do think that decisions are physical, but they also think that beliefs and desires and fears are physical. Think, for instance, of your beliefs. If we endorse a materialistic, scientific view of humans, then we have to say that our beliefs are stored in our *brains*. In particular, they're coded in neural pathways. So they're *physical*. And so the materialistic, scientific view of humans is perfectly compatible with the idea that our decisions can be caused by our beliefs and desires and so on.

But the point I really want to make here is that advocates of the *spiritual*, *religious* view can say that our decisions are caused by our beliefs and desires and so on. Now, they presumably won't want to say that beliefs and desires are *physical* things, but despite this, they can still say that our decisions are caused by these things. For instance, they can say that Tracy's decision was caused by her fear of flying, and her belief that a train ticket would be less expensive, and her desire to see her mother, and so on.

It might be a bit hard to figure out what this sort of causation would *consist* in. After all, since advocates of the spiritual, religious view are committed to saying that beliefs and desires are nonphysical states of a nonphysical soul, and since they're also committed to saying that decisions are nonphysical actions of a nonphysical soul, it seems that they're going to have to maintain that the causation at issue here is a kind of *nonphysical* causation. And you might think that the idea of nonphysical causation is puzzling. Perhaps. But I want to assume for the sake of argument that this makes sense. I say this in the spirit of granting as much as I can to advocates of the spiritual, religious view. I'm not saying that they *have* to endorse the view that our decisions can be caused by beliefs and desires and so on. But I want to grant for the sake of argument that if advocates of the spiritual, religious view *want* to say that our decisions are caused by our beliefs and desires and so on, then they *can*.

OK, so that's a bit of background. I now want to show that the two arguments against free will—the random-or-predetermined argument and the scientific argument—still stand, even if we endorse a spiritual, religious view of humans. Let's start with the random-or-predetermined argument.

## The Random-or-Predetermined Argument Against Free Will (Spiritual-Religious Version)

Let's go back to your decision to order chocolate ice cream instead of vanilla. And let's assume for the sake of argument that you have a nonphysical soul. Nonetheless, even if you do have a nonphysical soul, we can still say that your decision was either caused by prior events or not caused by prior events. If it was caused by prior events, it was presumably caused by things like your beliefs and desires and so on. Perhaps you believed that eating chocolate has certain health benefits and that these benefits can counteract the unhealthiness of the sugar and fat in ice cream. Or perhaps you had a strong desire to have the wonderful sensation of delicious chocolaty goodness on your tongue. Or whatever. You presumably have a bunch of beliefs, desires, preferences, and so on that might be relevant to your decision, and the first point to note here is that these things either caused your decision to order chocolate ice cream or they didn't.

If your decision was indeed caused by your beliefs and desires and so on, then it wasn't a product of your free will because it was *predetermined*. In other words, in this scenario, your choice wasn't free because it was already determined what you were going to do *before* you made your conscious decision.

If, on the other hand, your decision *wasn't* caused by anything, then it just *happened*. In other words, it happened *randomly*. And as we've already seen, it makes no sense to say that you chose of your own free will if your decision occurred randomly, or if it *just happened*.

So it seems that either way, your decision wasn't a product of your free will. And this is true even if you have a nonphysical soul. Moreover, the same thing can be said about *all* of our decisions. Even if we all possess nonphysical souls, it is still true that our decisions are either caused by prior events or not caused by prior events. And so the random-or-predetermined argument against free will still stands, even if we assume that the spiritual, religious view of humans is right.

### The Scientific Argument Against Free Will (Spiritual-Religious Version)

It's even easier to see that the spiritual, religious view doesn't give us a way of blocking the *scientific* argument against free will. For even if we assume that we all have nonphysical souls, it's still true that people can be influenced by things like subliminal messages. And it's still true that neuroscientists could predict your behavior, before you make your decisions, by looking at your brain activity. We have scientific *evidence* for these claims. And they seem to tell against the idea that we have free will, regardless of whether we have nonphysical souls.

In fact, if anything, the neuroscientific findings seem to count as evidence against the spiritual, religious view of

Even if we all possess nonphysical souls, it is still true that our decisions are either caused by prior events or not caused by prior events.

humans. Think about it. If our brains are causing our actions before consciousness enters the picture, then what would the *point* of a nonphysical soul be? What would it be *doing*? I don't want to try to argue for this here, but it does seem that the neuroscientific findings undermine the *need* for a nonphysical soul.

But regardless of whether this is right, the main point here is that the belief in nonphysical souls doesn't seem to give us a response to the scientific argument against free will. Even if we have nonphysical souls, if it's really true that neuroscientists can predict our actions by looking at what's happening in our brains *before* we make our conscious decisions, then it's hard to see how it could be right to say that we have free will.

If the spiritual, religious view of humans doesn't give us a way of responding to the anti-free-will arguments, then we need to figure out whether there's some *other* way of responding to these arguments. And that's what the rest of this book is going to be about.

# CAN PHILOSOPHY SAVE FREE WILL?

Unlike psychologists and neuroscientists, most professional philosophers believe in free will. And most of them endorse the same response to the anti-free-will arguments. The view that these philosophers endorse is known as *compatibilism*. It's a very old view that goes back at least to the ancient Greek Stoics. And it was made very famous and popular by the eighteenth-century Scottish philosopher David Hume.

In a nutshell, compatibilism is the view that there is no incompatibility between free will and determinism. To help us get a better picture of this view, let's go back to your decision to order chocolate ice cream, and let's assume for the sake of argument that this decision was completely caused by prior events. In fact, let's assume that determinism is true, so that it was already settled that you were going to order chocolate ice cream 13 billion years ago, just after the Big Bang took place. Compatibilists like Hume think that even if this is true, it still makes perfect sense to say that you decided to order chocolate ice cream of your own free will.

At first glance, this is likely to seem completely insane, so let me do my best to make it seem believable. According to Hume, we need to start by asking what it *means* to say that you chose of your own free will. Hume thinks it can mean only one thing, namely:

You did what you *wanted* to do.

But what does it mean to say that you "did what you wanted to do"? Well, one seemingly reasonable thing to say about this is that if your desires (or your "wants") *generated* your action, or your decision, then you "did what you wanted to do"—and hence, according to Hume, you acted freely. If this is right—and Humean compatibilists think it is— then we're led to the following result:

If in general your decisions and actions are *caused by* your desires, then you have free will.

Now, in a way, this sounds very reasonable. In the case of your decision to order chocolate ice cream, let's suppose that your choice was caused by your desire to experience the rush of joy that always follows on the heels of the in- gestion of chocolate and/or chocolate substitutes. Then it would seem that you did exactly what you *wanted* to do, and so it seems reasonable to say that you chose of your own free will.

But now notice that if Hume is right about this, then free will is perfectly compatible with full-blown determinism. Let's suppose that every event is completely caused by prior events, so that once the Big Bang happened, it was already determined how the entire history of the universe would go. In particular, it was already determined that you were going to order chocolate ice cream when you got to the front of the line. Still, it's not as if the Big Bang *directly* caused your decision. It caused your decision indirectly, by means of a long causal chain. The Big Bang happened; and that caused another event to happen, call it E2; and then that caused a third event to happen, E3; and so on. Eventually, 13 billion years later, at the end of the causal chain, something caused you to have a *desire* for a certain heavenly chocolaty sensation. And then, finally, that desire caused you to order chocolate ice cream when you got to the front of the line. It was all completely caused. But still, your decision was caused by your own desire. And so you did what you *wanted* to do. And so, according to Hume, you were free in the only reasonable sense of the term.

This might make compatibilism seem a bit more plausible than it does when we first hear it. But still, at the end of the day, most people find this view pretty hard to swallow.

Now, as I said before, compatibilism is actually very popular among professional philosophers; indeed, a recent survey showed that 60 percent of professional philosophers endorse compatibilism. But as soon as you leave the philosophy department, it's hard to find people who take the view seriously. When nonphilosophers hear about compatibilism, their response is usually to dismiss the view as obviously false and, indeed, borderline psychotic. The idea that it could be right to say that you ordered chocolate ice cream of your own free will, even if your decision was causally predetermined by events that took place billions of years ago, just seems preposterous to most people.

But, of course, the philosophers who endorse compatibilism aren't impressed at all by this dismissive response to their view. In fact, in their eyes, this dismissiveness doesn't count as a *response* at all; it's just a flat denial of their view. Most compatibilists would say something like this:

Look, compatibilism might sound crazy when you first hear it, but you have to look at the argument for the view. If Hume's right that having free will is just a matter of being able to do what you want, then the truth of compatibilism follows by ironclad *logic*. So the only way that you can reject Humean compatibilism is to reject Hume's view of what free will *is*. But Hume's view here is extremely plausible. All he's saying is that free will is the ability to *do what you want*, or to *act on your desires*. So if you want to reject compatibilism, then you have to argue that Hume is in fact wrong about this.

And to this, let me add another point: Hume's view isn't the only version of compatibilism in the philosophical literature. There are many other versions, and most of them proceed in essentially the same way—by arguing for a certain definition of the term "free will" and then showing that if the given definition is correct, then free will is compatible with determinism. So if we want to argue against compatibilism—if we don't want to simply *dismiss* the view—then we have to argue that *none* of the various compatibilist definitions of "free will" is correct. And this could take some doing, because a number of the compatibilist definitions sound pretty plausible when you first hear them.

So we seem to be caught between a rock and a hard place. We seem to have to choose between just dismissing compatibilism as obviously false (and thus being deemed irrational by the professional philosophers who endorse the view) and engaging in a long, difficult argument about how the term "free will" is to be defined. But I think there's a third alternative. The trick is not to fall into the trap of trying to argue that compatibilism is *false*; the trick is to argue instead that it's *irrelevant*—that even if it's true, it simply doesn't matter.

To see why compatibilism is irrelevant, we need to distinguish two kinds of free will (actually, if we want to, we can distinguish *many* kinds of free will, but I'll be able to make my point by discussing only two of them). The first kind of free will is the kind that Hume has in mind—it's the ability to do what you want, or to act on your desires. Let's call this *Hume-style free will*. The second kind of free will is the kind that I've been talking about in this book. It's the kind that you have if your decisions are neither predetermined by prior events nor completely random. Let's call this *not-predetermined free will*, or for short, *NPD free will*.

Given the distinction between Hume-style free will and NPD free will, we can make the following four points:

1. Hume-style free will is obviously compatible with determinism; in other words, it's obviously compatible with the idea that all of our decisions are completely caused by events that occurred in the distant past.

2. NPD free will is obviously *not* compatible with determinism. In fact, it's built into the very *definition* of NPD free will that it's not compatible with determinism. That's why it's called *not-predetermined* free will.

3. Human beings obviously *have* Hume-style free will. This isn't even controversial. After all, Hume-

The trick is not to fall into the trap of trying to argue that compatibilism is *false*; the trick is to argue instead that it's *irrelevant*—that even if it's true, it simply doesn't matter.

style free will is just the ability to act on your desires. Anyone who's ever eaten a cookie because she wanted one *knows* that we have *this* kind of free will.[1]

4. It's not obvious at all whether we have NPD free will. Some people think it's an illusion; others think it's real. In short, there is a raging debate about whether we have NPD free will. In fact, the arguments against free will that we discussed in chapter 2—the scientific argument and the random-or-predetermined argument—are best thought of as arguments against NPD free will.

But given these four points, Hume's whole view seems completely unhelpful. All he's really done is pointed out the obvious—that Hume-style free will is compatible with determinism and that we have Hume-style free will. But this doesn't do anything to change the fact that there is an important open question about whether we have *NPD* free will.

Perhaps Hume would respond to this by saying that part of his point is that what I'm calling "Hume-style free will" is *real* free will. I'll respond to this in the same way that my teenage daughter responds to me when I tell her that she has to be home by midnight: *Whatever*. I just don't *care* what "real" free will is. In fact, I don't even know what it *means* to say that Hume-style free will is *real* free will. This sounds to me like a dispute about *words*. I don't care about the *expression* "free will." The question I care about is a question about *human beings*—it's the question of whether we have a certain, specific *kind* of free will, namely, what I'm calling NPD free will. But, frankly, I don't care what we call this kind of free will. If Hume wants to take the expression "free will" for his own, he can *have* it. I can use a different term. Indeed, at the moment, I *am* using a different term—I'm using "NPD free will." But, again, it doesn't matter whether we call it "NPD free will" or just "free will." All that matters is whether we *have* it. That's the important question about free will—the question of whether human beings have *not-predetermined* free will.

You might respond to this by claiming that even if NPD free will is important, Hume-style free will is important too. Well, I think that's right; I think it's extremely important that we have Hume-style free will, and I would never suggest otherwise. But the *question* of whether we have Hume-style free will is *not* important. This is simply because we already know the answer to that question. It's entirely *obvious* that we have Hume-style free will. The interesting question—and the controversial question— is whether we *also* have NPD free will. And the point I'm making here is that this question is interesting and important *regardless* of what we *call* this kind of free will.

Before moving on, I should say that this response to Hume is not new. Other philosophers have made similar points. For instance, the eighteenth-century German philosopher Immanuel Kant called Humean compatibilism "petty word jugglery" and a "wretched subterfuge." And the nineteenth-century American philosopher William James said this:

> [Compatibilism] is a quagmire of evasion under which the real issue of fact has been entirely smothered. ... No matter what the [compatibilist] means by ["free will"] ... there is a problem, an issue of fact and not of words.[2]

These are strong words. But notice that Kant and James are *not* saying that compatibilism is *false*. They're saying it's *irrelevant*. They're saying that compatibilists are just playing around with words and evading the real issue. And that's exactly what I'm saying.

I said a moment ago that the important question is whether we have NPD free will and that I don't care whether we use the expression "free will" to refer to this kind of freedom. But I should point out that in the rest of this book, I am going to do just that. I'm going to be discussing the question of whether we have NPD free will, and I'm going to use the term "free will" to talk about it. But this is just for convenience—because it would get really annoying to keep using the phrase "NPD free will."

# WHAT *IS* FREE WILL, ANYWAY?

In the last chapter, we distinguished two kinds of free will—Hume-style free will and not-predetermined free will. It's pretty obvious that we have Hume-style free will, but this isn't very interesting. The interesting question is whether we also have not-predetermined free will. This is the kind of free will that we *want but might not have*; and it's also the kind of free will that's come under fire recently from psychology and neuroscience.

In chapters 6 and 7, I'm going to discuss the question of whether we have this not-predetermined kind of free will; but before we get into this, we need to get a better understanding of what this kind of free will *consists* in—or more precisely, what it *would* consist in, if we had it. That's what this chapter will be about; I will provide a picture of what not-predetermined free will *is*, or what it *would be*. (And, again, I will usually drop the "not-predetermined" qualifier and just call it *free will*.)

Having a better understanding of this kind of free will is going to be crucial in the rest of this book. The scientists who argue against free will are often rather confused about what free will is supposed to be. And so it will be very important for us—when we go to evaluate the anti-free-will arguments—to have a clear, *un*confused picture of what free will would consist in, if indeed we had it. Therefore, I'm going to start out here by clearing up four confusions that are often present in discussions of free will. In particular, these confusions are often buried in the discussions of those who argue against free will.

## Four Confusions

### The First Confusion: Remnants of Spiritualism

The people who reject free will—mostly, psychologists and neuroscientists—almost always endorse the materialistic, scientific view of humans. In other words, they reject the view that we have nonphysical souls. But then when they talk about mental events like conscious *decisions*, they talk about the neural events that *realize* these decisions, or the neural *correlates* of our decisions.

This is an utter confusion. If you don't believe in nonphysical souls, then you have to say that a conscious decision *is* a neural event. You can't say that there's a conscious decision and then say that there's *also* a neural correlate of the decision, as if the neural event and the conscious decision are two different things. That's what religious people who believe in nonphysical souls should say. But when materialistic neuroscientists talk this way, they're just confused.

Let me make sure this point is clear. Think about the relationship between Mark Twain and Sam Clemens. Imagine someone saying that Mark Twain is the "literary correlate" of Sam Clemens. If we heard someone say this, we would scratch our heads and respond by saying something like this:

> What on God's green Earth are you talking about? Mark Twain *is* Sam Clemens. When you say that he's the "literary correlate" of Sam Clemens, it sounds like you think there are two different men that stand in some special relationship to one another. But, of course, there *aren't* two different men here. There's just *one*. The names "Mark Twain" and "Sam Clemens" are just two different names of the very same man.

If you don't believe in nonphysical souls, then this is exactly what you have to say about your conscious decision to order chocolate ice cream and its so-called "neural correlate." You have to say that the conscious decision just *is* the neural event. There aren't two different things here; there are just two different ways of describing a single event. You can call it a "neural event" or a "conscious decision," but when you do this, you're just giving two different descriptions of the same thing.

It's easy to see that if you endorse the materialistic, scientific view of humans, then you're *forced* to accept this view. Think about it. A conscious decision has to be either a *physical* event or a *nonphysical* event. But if you endorse the materialistic, scientific view of humans, you obviously can't say that it's nonphysical. You *have* to say it's physical. But if a conscious decision is a physical event, then it has to be a *neural* event. What else could it be? There are no other physical events in your head that could possibly be decisions.

### The Second Confusion: The Locus of Free Will

People who argue against free will are often in a state of total confusion about where exactly free will is supposed to be located. In other words, they're confused about the exact times, during the course of your day, that you're supposed to be exercising your free will. And what's more, they're extremely *careless* about this issue. They write indiscriminately about having free will over what you *think*, what you *do*, and what you *choose*, as if these were all the same thing. But they're not the same thing. As we'll now see, they're importantly different.

The enemies of free will sometimes talk about having free will over your *thoughts*. They point out that we don't choose the ideas that occur to us, or that cross our minds, and in saying this, they think they're arguing that we don't have free will. But who in the world ever said that we *do* have free will over our thoughts? I don't know of a single advocate of free will, in the entire history of philosophy, who thinks that the problem of free will has to do with the stream of consciousness. We don't first decide what thoughts to think and *then* think them. We just *think* them. No one ever suggested otherwise. And there's a *reason* for this—it doesn't even *seem* that we have free will over our thoughts.

More importantly, who would *want* this kind of freedom? Imagine how hard it would be to solve a math problem if before you could think anything, you had to *decide* to think it. How *cumbersome* would that be? And how *annoying*? Or worse, what would it be like to fantasize about Marilyn Monroe or Brad Pitt if before you could have a thought, you had to decide to have that thought? If this were what free will amounted to, I wouldn't want it, and I don't think anyone else would either.

Given that the locus of free will isn't in our thoughts, the next suggestion might be that it's in our *actions*—that we have free will over what we *do*. This might be a *little* better than the idea that we have free will over our thoughts, but not much. Think of everything you do in a day. Just in the course of a single *minute*, you might perform twenty actions. Think, for instance, of what happens when you drive home from work or school. You get in the car; you put your seatbelt on; you put your key in the ignition; you turn the key; you push your foot down on the gas; you put the car in gear; you look in the mirror; and so on. We're almost *constantly* doing things. We barely even notice them. In fact, sometimes we don't seem to notice them at *all.* Thirty minutes after you turn your car on, you arrive at home. Along the way, you did all sorts of things. You accelerated numerous times, you hit the brake, you turned left, you turned right, you changed lanes, you got off the freeway at the right exit, you put your turn signal on, you scratched your face, and so on. You don't *remember* doing any of these things. And more importantly for our purposes, you didn't make conscious *decisions* to do them. We don't *decide* to do things like this, because we don't *need* to. And thank God. Imagine what a nightmare your life would be if you had to consciously decide to do everything you do. You could forget about talking to someone while taking a stroll. Your mind would be completely occupied with deciding how to move your legs. Here's a snapshot of what your thoughts might be like if you had to consciously decide to do everything you do:

> Move your left foot forward. OK, good, now your
> right. Left again. Right. Good God, man, look out for

that pothole. Do you want to sprain your ankle? OK, good. Now, your right foot again. Now, your left. And don't forget to swing your arms. For heaven's sake, what will the Wilsons think if they see you walking around with your arms perfectly still?

I'm pretty sure that if we had *this* kind of free will, the suicide rate would be considerably higher. No one in his right mind would want to have to make all of these decisions.

So free will isn't about what we think *or* what we do. The obvious next suggestion is that we're just supposed to have free will over our *conscious decisions* and nothing else. Now, actually, a conscious decision is just a certain kind of action, and so the suggestion here is that we're supposed to have free will over a certain *subset* of our actions (namely, our conscious decisions). But even this is too broad. To see why, consider the following conversation:

> *Lucy*    Hey, Charlie, would you like me to jab this fork into your throat? I mean, it's no problem for *me*; I don't mind doing it at all. But I don't know if you want a fork in your throat, so it's up to you.

> *Charlie*    No, I think I'll pass on that, Lucy. Thanks for thinking of me, but I choose *not* to have a fork jabbed into my throat.

Charlie just made a conscious decision. But his choice was presumably completely caused by his beliefs and desires and so on. In particular, he believed that having a fork jabbed into his throat would kill him, and he desired not to die. So he chose to pass on the whole fork-jab thing. But given that his choice was completely caused by his beliefs and desires and so on, Charlie wasn't exercising his free will in the sense that matters here, because his decision was predetermined. Of course, there was definitely a *kind* of free will that Charlie was exercising in this case; in particular, he was exercising *Hume*-style free will. Recall from chapter 4 that Hume-style free will is just the ability to *do what you want*, or to *act on your desires*. But as we've already seen, this isn't the kind of free will that we're concerned with in this book. We're not concerned with the question of whether human beings have Hume-style free will; we're concerned with the question of whether they have *not-predetermined* free will. This is the kind of free will that we *want but might not have*.

But now notice that when it comes to decisions like Charlie's, we *don't* want not-predetermined free will. In cases like this, we want our desires to completely cause our choices. Or at any rate, that's what you *should* want. If you said that you *didn't* want this, you'd be saying that you want it to be the case that you *might* tell Lucy to jab the fork into your throat, despite the fact that you don't *want* her to do this. But that's crazy. Surely what we want here is for our desire to avoid death to cause us to choose in the right way. In other words, in cases like this, all we want is *Hume*-style free will. We don't want not-predetermined free will.

So the conclusion of all of this is that it's not quite right to say that the locus of free will (or the kind of free will that we're talking about here) is our conscious decisions. There are *some* kinds of conscious decisions (namely, decisions like Charlie's) where we don't have free will and don't want it.

We're finally ready to say where we *do* want free will. Or better, we're ready to say where we want to have *not-predetermined* free will. We want it in connection with a certain *subset* of our conscious decisions. In particular, we want it in connection with what we can call *torn* decisions. Torn decisions can be defined as follows:

> A *torn decision* is a conscious decision in which you have multiple options and you're torn as to which option is best. More precisely, you have multiple options that seem to you to be more or less tied for best, so that you feel completely unsure—or entirely torn—as to what you ought to do. And you decide *while* feeling torn.

Let me make three quick points about torn decisions. First of all, notice that I'm only talking here about decisions that you make *while* feeling torn. Sometimes we start off feeling torn but then we think about the situation for a while, and we come up with reasons for favoring one of our options, and we no longer feel torn. In cases like this, you're not making a torn decision. Rather, you're making a decision that started off looking like it might be torn but then turned out not to be. In contrast to this, a torn decision occurs when you decide while you're still torn. For instance, in the ice cream case, you might decide while feeling utterly torn between chocolate and vanilla. And the reason you would want to choose while still feeling torn should be obvious; if you got to the front of the line, and everyone was waiting, it would make a lot more sense to make a torn decision—that is, to *just choose*—than it would to keep on deliberating, or to just stand there until it became clear to you which flavor you wanted.

Second, it's important to remember that torn decisions are always *conscious* decisions. So we have to distinguish torn decisions from what might be called torn *actions*. I'm thinking here of cases where we're in "torn situations" and we settle them without stopping to think about it, and without making a conscious decision. Here are two examples of this:

(i) You're driving down the street when a child suddenly runs in front of your car. You don't have time to stop, but you can avoid hitting the child by jerking the wheel to the left or the right and there's no obvious reason for choosing either option. You jerk the wheel to the left without consciously deciding to do so. In other words, you just *react*.

(ii) You go to the grocery store to get a can of Campbell's tomato soup. There are five nearly identical cans lined up next to each other on the shelf—yes, just like the Andy Warhol painting (you're very clever)—and you grab one of the cans without pausing to think about which one you should take.

We don't exercise our free will in cases like these, and once again, we should thank our lucky stars that we don't *have* to. In cases like (i), it would be bad to have to exercise our free will because in order to do this we would have to act *consciously*, and as psychologists and neuroscientists have shown in numerous studies, consciousness is very *slow*. When you're in an emergency situation (or when you're playing basketball or something like that), you don't want to have to engage your conscious mind. It's much better to have the ability to simply *react*, unconsciously. As for (ii), we don't want free will in cases like this either, but the reason is different. It's because it would be *boring*. No one wants to have to stop and think about which can of Campbell's soup to buy, because we don't *care*—it just doesn't matter which one we buy. We only want to engage our free will when we're faced with torn situations that we care about. So, for instance, if you're faced with a choice between tomato soup and mushroom soup, and if you're torn as to which one to get, then you *do* want to engage your conscious free will. But you don't want to bother doing this when you're picking between two identical cans of tomato soup. You'd look like an imbecile, standing there in the aisle of the supermarket waffling between the two cans, weighing them in your hands to see whether perhaps one of them had a bit more soup in it.

Third, it's important to be clear about *how often* we make torn decisions. The answer, I think, is several times a day. Think about a normal day. You might make torn decisions about whether to have eggs or cereal for breakfast. Or whether to drive to work or ride your bike. Or if you're driving, whether to take surface streets or the freeway. Or whether to work through lunch or eat with your friend Andre. Or whether to go to a movie in the evening or stay home. Or if you're in a restaurant, you might make a torn decision about which entrée to order.

But while we make several torn decisions a day, it's not as if we're *constantly* making them. If you're watching a movie, or talking to a friend on the phone, or driving home from work on "auto-pilot," you're not making torn decisions. But if you think about an ordinary day, I think you'll notice that you make torn decisions fairly often. We seem to make at least a few of them every day.

So the picture that's emerging here is that of a person plodding through her day without exercising her free will, and then every once in a while—sometimes once an hour, sometimes less, sometimes more—she comes to a fork in the road, and she has to make a torn decision as to which way to go. She chooses one of the two roads, and then she plods on, without exercising her free will until she comes to another fork in the road. This is represented graphically in figure 1.

In the diagram in figure 1, the long line represents the path that the person has taken through life. The dots represent torn decisions. The short lines coming out of the dots represent paths that the person could have taken but didn't. And here's my claim: *We want free will at the dots and the dots only.* These are the only places where we *need* free will, and they're the only places where we *want* free will. Or more precisely, the dots are the only places where we need and want *not-predetermined* free will.

Let me say one more thing about torn decisions before moving on. The examples of torn decisions that I've mentioned here are all pretty unimportant. They're about things like whether to have soup or salad with your dinner. So you might conclude from this that the whole topic of torn decisions is unimportant. But don't be fooled. First of all, some of our torn decisions can be very important. For instance, you might have a good job offer in a city you hate,

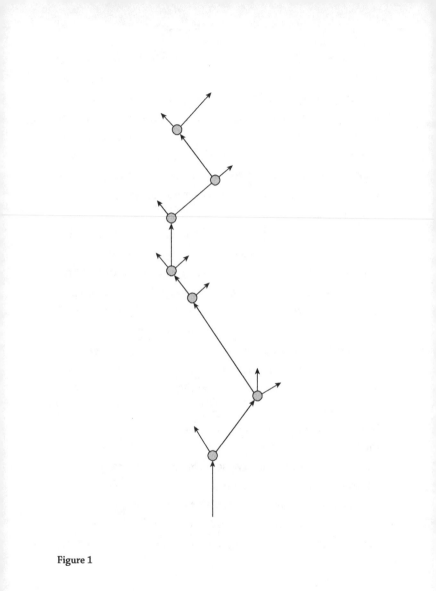

**Figure 1**

and you might be utterly torn and have to decide without knowing what you should do. Second, even though a single, individual torn decision can seem very unimportant, the sum total of *all* of these decisions starts to seem important. If you didn't have control over *any* of the little decisions that you made in your life, that would be tantamount to saying that you didn't have control over your *life*. Having free will is largely about having free will over a whole bunch of little decisions. And finally, while these little torn decisions can seem unimportant while you're lying on the couch reading about free will, when you're actually in the *moment*—when you're about to make a torn decision—it doesn't *feel* unimportant. Imagine, for instance, that you're in a fancy restaurant, and there are two items on the menu that look really good to you. You're torn as to which one to order. Of course, there's a sense in which it doesn't really matter what you get. After all, you'll be dead in a hundred years anyway. But the fact of the matter is that we *do* care about decisions like this. When the waiter comes to the table and you're about to choose, you *care*. And when you're at the theater trying to decide whether to see *Death Blow* or *Rochelle, Rochelle*, you care again. And I would argue that you *should* care. Who wants to go through life not caring about stuff like this? You'd be bored out of your mind. I mean, come on; what the hell else is there to care about?

**The Third Confusion: Only a Certain Feature of Our Torn
Decisions Needs to Be Undetermined**

Let's go back to your decision to order chocolate ice cream,
and let's suppose now that it was a *torn* decision, that when
you decided to order chocolate ice cream, you were feeling
utterly torn about whether to get chocolate or vanilla. We
already know that in order for this decision to have been
a product of your free will, it needs to be that it wasn't
completely caused, or predetermined, by prior events. But
it's important to notice that only a certain *feature* of the
decision needs to have been undetermined. To appreciate
this, consider the following possibility:

> *Possible state of affairs*    When you got to the front of
> the line, you were definitely going to order some ice
> cream. You were hungry, and you had been looking
> forward to having ice cream all day, and there was
> just no question about it—you were going to order
> some ice cream. In fact, in the possible scenario I'm
> imagining, your desires *completely caused* you to
> order ice cream. Now, when you first got in line, you
> noticed that there were thirty-one flavors to choose
> from. But while you waited, you ruled out twenty-
> nine of those flavors for various reasons. You ruled
> out Espresso Swirl because it reminded you of your
> pretentious boss, who's always drinking espresso
> out of those stupid little cups with his idiotic pinkie

sticking out like he just popped out of a Jane Austen novel. And you ruled out Double-Fat Fudge because while you're not exactly wild about fat-free ice cream, you didn't see any need to turn your dessert into a statement about how comfortable you are with your body. And you ruled out Bubble Gum Surprise because ... well, because it *sucks*. And so on. In short, your various beliefs and desires and preferences *completely caused* you to rule out those twenty-nine flavors. But you couldn't make up your mind whether to order chocolate or vanilla, and you eventually chose while feeling utterly torn. And finally, nothing caused your decision to be a chocolate-over-vanilla choice.

Of course, this is all just a *possibility*. But it brings up an important point. There are various features of a torn decision that can be uncaused, and for all we know, it could be that some of these features are completely uncaused whereas others are completely predetermined. In particular, it makes perfect sense to say that (a) your beliefs and desires and preferences completely caused you to rule out the first twenty-nine flavors, and (b) they completely caused you to make a torn decision between chocolate and vanilla, and (c) *nothing* caused you to choose chocolate over vanilla.

Now, here's the really important point for us: the only thing that matters to the issue of free will is point (c). In other words, in order for a torn decision to be a product of my free will, the only thing that needs to be undetermined is *which tied-for-best option was chosen*. It's perfectly fine if everything else about the decision was completely caused by prior events.

**The Fourth Confusion: Different Kinds of Randomness**
The fourth and final confusion I want to discuss is perhaps the most important. It has to do with the fact that there are multiple ways in which an event can be "random."

One thing we might mean when we say that an event is random is that it's *unpredictable*. For instance, if we're playing roulette in Las Vegas, we might say that where the ball lands is completely random. When we say this, all we mean is that it's unpredictable.

Second, one might use the term "random" to mean *uncaused*. If an event isn't caused by anything, then it *just happens*, and so there's a sense in which it happens *randomly*. (This is the sense of "random" that seems to be at play in the random-or-predetermined argument against free will.)

There's a third sense of "random" that seems relevant to torn decisions. If I ask you *why* you chose chocolate over vanilla, you might say something like this: "I don't know; I didn't really have a reason; I just picked it." In this scenario, it seems to make sense to say that you chose *randomly*, or *arbitrarily*. When we say this, what we mean is that you didn't have a *reason* for your choice. Of course, you *did* have reasons for wanting to order chocolate ice cream, but you *also* had reasons for wanting to order vanilla ice cream, and the point here is that you didn't have an *all-things-considered* reason for *preferring* chocolate to vanilla. And given this—given that you made a *torn* decision—it makes sense to say that you chose randomly, or arbitrarily, and so, again, this gives us a third sense of the word "random."

But it's not obvious that any of these kinds of randomness are the ones that are relevant to the issue of free will. Remember, we already know that free will requires a kind of nonrandomness. I've pointed out a few times that if a decision occurs randomly, then it can't be the product of your free will. But what *kind* of randomness are we talking about here? In other words, what kind of *non*randomness is needed for free will? The answer, it seems to me, is as follows:

> For a decision to be the product of my free will, it can't be that the decision just *happened to me*. It has to be that *I made* the decision. In other words, the decision has to be *mine*. I have to have been the *author* of the decision.

This gives us a *fourth* kind of randomness. To say that a decision is random in this sense is to say that it wasn't *me* who made the decision, that the decision just happened to me. I think that this is the kind of randomness that's relevant to free will.

Why do I say this? Why is this the kind of randomness that matters to free will? We can see why this is so by looking at four sentences that correspond to the four different kinds of randomness. Three of the sentences are going to make perfect sense, but the fourth one is going to be an incoherent contradiction in terms. Here are the four sentences:

> *Sentence 1* "I chose of my own free will, and no one could have *predicted* that I was going to choose chocolate over vanilla."

> *Sentence 2* "I chose of my own free will, and nothing *caused* me to choose in the way that I did; in other words, nothing *made* me choose chocolate over vanilla; I just *did* choose that way."

> *Sentence 3* "I chose of my own free will, but I didn't have a *reason* for choosing chocolate over vanilla; in other words, I was completely torn between those two options, and I just *arbitrarily* chose to order chocolate over vanilla."

> *Sentence 4* "I chose of my own free will, but it wasn't *me* who chose; rather, the choice just *happened* to me."

Here's what I want to say: sentences 1 through 3 make perfect sense, but sentence 4 is incoherent. It simply makes no sense at all to say that I chose of my own free will but it wasn't *me* who chose. This is just a contradiction. But it *does* make sense to say—as sentences 1 through 3 do—that I chose of my own free but nothing *made* me choose as I did, and I had no *reason* for choosing as I did, and no one could have predicted how I was going to choose.

What this shows is that it's the fourth kind of randomness that's incompatible with free will. In other words, the kind of nonrandomness that's required for free will is the kind that has to do with it being *me* who chose.

## A Picture of Free Will

If what I just said about randomness is right, it gives us a better understanding of what free will *is*. Or at any rate, it gives us a better understanding of the kind of free will that we're concerned with here, namely, *not-predetermined* free will. So far we've found that for a decision to be free in this sense, it has to satisfy two conditions: first, it can't be *predetermined*, and second, it can't be *random*. But now that we know more about the kind of randomness that we're talking about here, we can be more precise about what this sort of free will amounts to. In particular, we can say this:

*Not-predetermined free will*    For a decision to be a product of my free will (in the sense of *not-predetermined* free will, as opposed to *Hume*-style free will), two things need to be true. First, it needs to have been *me* who made the decision; and second, my choice needs to have not been predetermined by prior events. In other words, it needs to be the case that (a) *I* did it, and (b) nothing *made* me do it.

That's what free will is. Or rather, this is what free will *would* be, if in fact we have it. But, of course, the jury is still out on whether we actually have this kind of free will.

A second important lesson that we've learned about free will in this chapter is that it's not something that we exercise *continuously*. In other words, if we have free will, then we only exercise it *intermittently*, at certain specific moments. In particular, we only exercise free will (if we have it at all) when we make *torn decisions*—when we're in situations where we're confronted with multiple options that seem equally good to us, and we stop and think for at least a brief moment about what we should do, and then we settle the matter with a conscious *choosing*. That's it. We don't exercise free will (and we don't need to or want to) at any other time.

The last point I want to make here is that the picture of free will that I've painted in this chapter is perfectly compatible with both the materialistic, scientific view of humans and the spiritual, religious view. What I've said here, in a nutshell, is that for a decision to be a product of my

So far we've found that for a decision to be free in this sense, it has to satisfy two conditions: first, it can't be *predetermined*, and second, it can't be *random*.

free will, it needs to be the case that (a) *I* did it, and (b) nothing *made* me do it. This, I think, is what you should say, whether you believe in nonphysical souls or not. Of course, if you endorse a materialistic view, you'll say that conscious decisions are physical *brain* events, whereas if you endorse a spiritualistic view, you'll presumably want to say that conscious decisions are nonphysical actions of nonphysical souls. But either way, you should say that for a decision of mine to be *free*, it needs to be the case that *I* did it and nothing *made* me do it. That's just what free will *is*. Or, again, to be more precise, it's what (not-predetermined) free will would be, if we have it.

# CAN WE BLOCK THE RANDOM-OR-PREDETERMINED ARGUMENT AGAINST FREE WILL?

Now that we know what free will would consist in, we need to move on to the task of figuring out whether we actually have it. The problem, of course, is that the two arguments against free will (the scientific argument and the random-or-predetermined argument) still stand. And what's more, the two main responses to the anti-free-will arguments—the religious response and the philosophical response—don't work. So the question we need to ask is whether there's some *other* way of responding to these arguments.

I'll start by discussing the random-or-predetermined argument. It makes sense to start with this argument because it's an attempt to show that free will is downright impossible. This is very different from the scientific argument, which just tries to show (by presenting empirical evidence) that we don't actually *have* free will. But if free will is impossible—if the whole notion of free will is *incoherent*—then there's little reason to bother looking at the empirical data.

Let's start by recalling how the random-or-predetermined argument proceeds. It goes like this:

*The random-or-predetermined argument against free will* For each different conscious decision you've made in your life, we can say for certain that it was either caused by prior events or not caused by prior events. But if a decision *was* caused by prior events, then it wasn't a product of your free will, because it was already determined by things that happened before you chose. And if a decision *wasn't* caused by prior events, then it wasn't a product of your free will, because it happened *randomly*, and it makes no sense to say that you chose of your own free will if your choice just randomly appeared in your brain.

The first half of this argument seems right. If your torn decisions are completely caused by prior events, then they're not the products of your free will (or at any rate, they're not the products of your free will in the sense that we're concerned with in this book). But I think the second half of the argument is confused. If nothing caused you to choose chocolate over vanilla, that might mean that your decision was random in *some* sense of the term, but it doesn't follow that it was random in the sense that matters to free will. The sense of randomness that's relevant to the issue of free will is the sense that has to do with whether it was *you* who made the decision. But even if we suppose that nothing caused you to choose chocolate over vanilla, it simply doesn't follow that it wasn't *you* who chose. And so it doesn't follow that you didn't choose of your own free will.

This point is crucial, so let me say a bit more to argue for it. Imagine that a team of neuroscientists scanned your brain while you were at the ice cream parlor, looking for the cause of your decision. And suppose that later on, the following conversation took place:

*Sally* Hey, did those neuroscientists figure out what caused you to choose chocolate over vanilla?

*You* Actually, they figured out that *nothing* caused me to do that. They found that my desire to eat ice cream (together with my inability to make up my mind over which flavor to order) caused me to make a torn decision between chocolate and vanilla. But *nothing* caused the decision to be a chocolate-over-vanilla decision. I could just as easily have chosen vanilla over chocolate.

So far, so good. But now suppose that Sally responded to you by saying this:

*Sally*    Wow. So I guess you didn't choose of your own free will.

It seems to me that this would be an utterly bizarre thing for Sally to say. In fact, I think that if she said this, it would make perfect sense for you to respond as follows:

*You*    What are you talking about? It was still *my* choice. All the neuroscientists discovered is that nothing caused me to choose chocolate over vanilla. But it doesn't follow that it wasn't *me* who chose. And so it doesn't follow that I didn't choose of my own free will.

I think this response is spot on. It seems to make perfect sense to say, "You chose chocolate over vanilla of your own free will, but nothing caused you to do that." Therefore, since this makes perfect sense, if we discovered that your choice was uncaused, we couldn't infer that you didn't choose of your own free will. And so it seems to me that the second half of the random-or-predetermined argument is simply mistaken.

The enemies of free will might respond to this by saying something like the following:

If it's true that literally *nothing* caused your choice to be a chocolate-over-vanilla choice, then one thing we can say is that *you* didn't cause it to be a chocolate-over-vanilla choice. In other words, you didn't *make this happen*. But then how could it be you who *did* it? It seems that it couldn't. It seems that if nothing caused this to happen—if nothing *made* it happen—then it *just happened*. In other words, it wasn't *you* at all.

If you feel inclined to respond in this way, then you have very likely forgotten a point that I made above—what in chapter 5 I called the "first confusion." The first confusion consisted in the idea that conscious decisions are somehow *different* from the corresponding neural events. They're not. If the materialistic, scientific view of humans is right, then conscious decisions just *are* neural events. So when you decided to order chocolate ice cream, a certain physical event occurred in your brain. In particular, it was a *neural* event. But it was *also* a conscious choosing event. More specifically, it was a *you-choosing-chocolate* event. That's what it *was*. In its very essence, it was a conscious decision of *yours*. Now let's suppose that nothing caused this event to be a chocolate-over-vanilla decision. That's fine. But this doesn't do anything to change the fact that it was a *you-consciously-choosing* event.

So it seems to me just confused to say that if nothing caused you to choose chocolate, then *you* didn't choose chocolate. Of course you did. We know for sure and certain that you chose chocolate. That's what the neural event in your head *was*—a you-consciously-choosing-chocolate event.

You might not have noticed this, but something kind of magical just happened. We didn't just refute the random-or-predetermined argument; we turned it completely upside-down. In other words, we just argued for the exact opposite conclusion. The central claim in the random-or-predetermined argument (or at any rate, the second half of that argument) was this:

> If our decisions are uncaused, then they're random, and so they're not the products of our free will.

We have now found that this claim is false. But that's not all. We've also found that the following (diametrically opposed) claim is true:

> If our torn decisions are uncaused, then when we make these decisions, nothing makes us choose in the ways that we do, and so they *are* the products of our free will.

Why is this true? Because in order for your torn decisions to be the products of your free will, two conditions need to be satisfied. It needs to be the case that (a) your torn

So it seems to me just confused to say that if nothing caused you to choose chocolate, then *you* didn't choose chocolate.

decisions are made *by you*, and (b) when you make your torn decisions, nothing *makes* you choose as you do. Now, we already *know* that condition (a) is satisfied; your torn decisions are definitely made *by you* because what they *are*, in their very essence, are you-consciously-choosing events. So the only real question is whether condition (b) is satisfied; in other words, the question is whether anything *makes* you choose as you do when you make your torn decisions. But if your torn decisions are uncaused, then it follows for certain that nothing makes you choose as you do. Thus, we are led to the conclusion that *if your torn decisions are uncaused, then they are the products of your free will*.

So we have now made significant progress. In particular, we have accomplished two things. First, we have refuted the random-or-predetermined argument against free will (because we have refuted the claim that if our torn decisions are uncaused then they're not free). And second, we have uncovered what the free will debate *turns* on. Why? Because we have found that both of the following are true:

1. If our torn decisions *are* caused by prior events, then we *don't* have free will.

2. If our torn decisions are *not* caused by prior events, then we *do* have free will.

So it seems that the free will debate comes down to the question of whether our torn decisions are caused by prior events.[1]

This is interesting. What it means is that the question of whether we have free will is a question for empirical science. Now, assuming that we *want* free will, this could be dangerous; it means that the right kind of scientific study could establish that we *don't* have free will.

Indeed, we've already seen that some people think that this has already happened. The enemies of free will have produced a powerful empirical-scientific argument for thinking that our decisions *are* caused by prior events and, hence, that we *don't* have free will. This is what we have called the *scientific* argument.

We still have to assess this argument, but the considerations of the present chapter suggest that the enemies of free will—or more specifically, the people who have articulated the scientific argument against free will—are at least on the right track. In other words, they are thinking about the problem correctly. The question of whether we have free will *is* a scientific question, and in particular, it *is* a question about whether our decisions are caused by prior events. So if the enemies of free will are right when they say that the evidence shows that our decisions are completely caused by prior events, then the game is over—we don't have free will.

Before I conclude this chapter, I want to point out that the response that I've given here to the random-or-predetermined argument against free will can be used by *all* of us, whether we believe in nonphysical souls or not—or in other words, whether we accept the spiritual, religious view of humans or the materialistic, scientific view. I have been assuming in my discussion that the materialistic, scientific view of humans is right. But advocates of the spiritual, religious view can say essentially the same things that I've said here. In particular, they can respond to the random-or-predetermined argument by saying something like this:

> If your torn decisions aren't caused by prior events, it doesn't follow that they aren't the products of your free will. On the contrary, in this scenario, they *are* the products of your free will, because (a) they're made *by you* (because they're you-consciously-choosing events that occur in your soul), and (b) when you make these decisions, nothing *makes* you choose in the ways that you do.

This, of course, is exactly analogous to the response to the random-or-predetermined argument that I have given here on behalf of those who endorse the materialistic, scientific view of humans. So what this means is that regardless of whether we believe in nonphysical souls, we can give essentially the same response to the random-or-predetermined argument against free will.

# CAN WE BLOCK THE SCIENTIFIC ARGUMENT AGAINST FREE WILL?

It's finally time to assess the scientific argument against free will and to decide whether it gives us a good reason to deny the existence of free will. In a nutshell, the scientific argument proceeds as follows:

> *The scientific argument against free will*     There is strong scientific evidence (from psychology and neuroscience) that supports the claim that our so-called conscious decisions are completely caused by events that occur *before* we choose, and which are completely out of our control, and indeed, which we're completely unaware of.

There are actually a few arguments here—one based on findings from psychology, and a couple of others based on findings from neuroscience. The argument from psychology is the least troubling, so let's start with that one.

## The Argument from Psychology

Let's begin by recalling how the argument from psychology goes. The argument is based on the fact that many of our actions and decisions are caused by things that we're completely unaware of—things like subliminal messages. Moreover, when this happens, people are often completely mistaken about why they did whatever it was that they did. They construct elaborate theories about the reasons for their actions; they believe that these theories are true, but from the outside, we can see that they aren't true at all. In short, the main idea behind the argument from psychology is that our actions are often caused by unconscious factors that are completely out of our control.

Given the discussion in chapter 5 about what free will *is*, we are now much better situated to see what might be wrong with this argument. The first point to make here is that most of the studies that psychologists have performed on this topic have been centrally concerned with our *behavior*—in other words, with things that we *do*. But as we saw in chapter 5, free will doesn't really have anything to do with our behavior. It has to do with our conscious *decisions*. In fact, on the view I've been developing, we're only supposed to exercise our free will when we're making *torn* decisions—decisions that we make while we're feeling torn as to which option is best. Now, it turns out that almost *none* of the psychological studies that we're talking about here are concerned with torn decisions, and so you might think that these studies are just irrelevant to the question of free will. But I think this would be too quick. For when we put all of the psychological studies together—when we look at them as a whole—they provide ample evidence for the following conclusion:

Our actions—across a whole spectrum of kinds of cases—are often influenced by unconscious factors that are completely out of our control.

The evidence for this is so widespread and so overwhelming, that it seems to follow that the phenomenon we're talking about here—the phenomenon of unconscious causes of our actions—almost certainly extends to our torn decisions. In other words, even if very few of the studies are explicitly concerned with torn decisions, the sum total of the studies suggests that human actions of *all different kinds* can be caused by unconscious factors that are completely out of our control. And so it stands to reason that torn decisions can be caused by unconscious factors as well.

But the psychological studies don't show—in fact, they don't even come *close* to showing—that our torn decisions are *always* caused by unconscious factors. And this is what they would need to do in order to show that we don't have free will. Think about it. If you believe in free will, you don't have to say *all* of your torn decisions are the products of your free will. You only have to say that *some* of them are. Suppose that you make, on average, five torn decisions a day. And now suppose that, on average, two of these decisions are caused by unconscious factors—in other words, by things that you're completely unaware of and that are completely out of your control. For instance, maybe you decided to order chocolate ice cream because you subconsciously hate your mother (because, unbeknownst to you, when you were a toddler, she used to bite your fingers and toes until they bled) and because the color of the vanilla ice cream subconsciously reminded you of her teeth. And maybe you bought a Coke at lunch because you were subconsciously motivated by some stupid billboard you saw on your way to work without even realizing it. Still, that leaves *three other* torn decisions that you made today. And maybe those decisions *weren't* caused by unconscious factors.

So the real question is this: have the studies that psychologists have performed here—the studies on things like subliminal messages—given us good reason to think that *whenever* we make torn decisions, our choices are *always* caused or predetermined by unconscious factors (in other words, by things that we're not aware of and that are out of our control)?

The answer to this question should be obvious. It's a resounding *no*. In fact, psychologists haven't come anywhere *near* establishing this result. All they've shown is that *sometimes* our actions are caused by things that we're not aware of.

The conclusion, then, is that the psychological studies on subconscious motivations—on things like subliminal messaging—don't show that we don't have free will. At most, they show that we exercise our free will a bit less often than we might have thought.

### The Arguments from Neuroscience

The last question we have to answer is whether the arguments from neuroscience succeed in showing that we don't have free will. But before we get into this, we need to answer an important preliminary question.

### A Preliminary Question: Is Neuroscience a Deterministic Science or a Probabilistic Science?

Back in chapter 2, I explained that quantum mechanics contains probabilistic laws. In other words, it contains laws that look like this:

If you have a physical system in state S, and if you perform experiment E on that system, then there are two different possible outcomes, namely, O1 and O2; moreover, there's a 50 percent chance that you'll get outcome O1 and a 50 percent chance that you'll get outcome O2.

This means that quantum mechanics allows for the possibility that some physical events are not predetermined. This is extremely important for the topic of free will because it opens the door to the possibility that our *torn decisions* are not predetermined.

But even if we assume that some physical events are not predetermined, it doesn't follow that any *neural* events are not predetermined. And that's the really important question for us. After all, assuming that the materialistic, scientific view of humans is correct, torn decisions just *are* neural events. Therefore, since the claim that we have free will depends on the claim that some of our torn decisions are not predetermined, it also depends on the claim that some *neural events* are not predetermined.

So what does current neuroscience tell us about this? Does it tell us that all neural events are completely predetermined by prior events? Or does it leave open the possibility that there are some neural events that are not predetermined? The answer is that it leaves open the possibility of indeterminism. In other words, current neuroscientific theory is *not* completely deterministic. Indeed, some of the most fundamental neural processes are treated probabilistically by neuroscience. Let me explain this in a bit more detail.

A *neuron* is a long, skinny cell that transmits information electronically. It's sort of like a telephone wire in the brain. But unlike telephone wires, distinct neurons are separated by tiny *gaps*. When an electrical signal travels down a neuron and reaches the end of the cell, a tiny particle (called a *neurotransmitter*) is released. The neurotransmitter travels across the gap to the next neuron. And when the neurotransmitter arrives at the next neuron, it causes that next neuron to *fire*—in other words, it causes an electrical signal to travel down *that* neuron, thus repeating the whole process all over again.

Notice that there are *two* main events here. One is the *release* of the little particle, or the neurotransmitter (this event is caused by the electrical signal arriving at the end of the neuron). The second event here is the *neural firing* (this is caused by the arrival of the neurotransmitter).

Now, here's the really important point for us: current neuroscientific theory treats *both* of these processes probabilistically. In other words, as far as our current theory is concerned, there are no deterministic laws that govern these processes. We do not have a law that says that *whenever* a neurotransmitter arrives at a neuron, it fires; and we also don't have a law that says that *whenever* a neuron fires, it triggers the release of a neurotransmitter. On the contrary, sometimes when a neuron fires, a neurotransmitter *isn't* released. And likewise, sometimes when a neurotransmitter arrives at a neuron, it doesn't fire. Finally, as far as neuroscience is concerned, it may be that specific events of these kinds are *not predetermined*. In other words, for all we know, it could be that in specific cases, whether a neuron fires (or whether a neurotransmitter is released) is not predetermined.

This is good news if you're hoping that we have free will. It means that as far as current neuroscientific theory is concerned, it may be that some neural events are not predetermined. And since this is something that's needed for free will, it seems that the door is at least open for the possibility of free will.

(Just to be clear, I'm not saying that neuroscientists have shown that there *are* neural events that are not predetermined. Rather, they have located certain kinds of neural events that, for all we know right now, *might* not be predetermined. In other words, the point is that neuroscientists haven't been able to find any evidence that the neural events in question are completely caused, or predetermined.)

But this is all extremely general. All it tells us is that it could be that some neural events are not predetermined. It doesn't tell us anything about torn decisions in particular. And the problem is that there are neuroscientific studies out there (in particular, the studies of Benjamin Libet and J. D. Haynes) that suggest that our torn decisions *are* predetermined, that they're completely caused by prior neural events that we're unaware of. So let's look and see whether these studies really do show what people say they show—namely, that we don't have free will.

**The Libet Studies**

The most famous of the neuroscientific arguments against free will is the one that's based on Libet's studies. Let's recall how this argument goes.

We have known for a long time (since the 1960s) that conscious decisions are associated with a certain kind of brain activity known as the _readiness potential_. In the early 1980s, Libet set out to establish a timeline for the readiness potential, the conscious intention to act, and the act itself. He had subjects face a large clock that could measure time in milliseconds, and he told them to flick their wrists whenever they felt an urge to do so and to note the exact time that they felt the conscious urge to move. What Libet found was that the readiness potential—the physical brain activity associated with our decisions—arose about a half a second before the conscious intention to move.

People have taken Libet's findings to show that we don't have free will. As I noted in chapter 2, the argument for this can be put in the following way:

> When you perform an action, if you don't make a conscious decision to act until _after_ the physical causes of your action have already been set in motion,

then the idea that you have free will is an illusion. It simply makes no sense to say that you decided to flick your wrist of your own free will if the physical causes of your action were already in motion before you made your conscious choice.

In other words, the idea here is that it can't be that we have free will—it can't be that our conscious decisions are the ultimate causes of our actions—because there are purely physical, nonconscious *brain* events that cause our actions and that occur *before* we make our conscious decisions.

That's the argument. And now I want to tell you what's *wrong* with it. In a nutshell, the problem with this argument is that it just *assumes* that the readiness potential plays a certain kind of causal role in the production of our actions. But, in fact, we have no idea what the purpose of the readiness potential is. We don't know *why* it occurs, and we don't know what it *does*.

This is an extremely important point. In order for Libet's findings to create a genuine problem for free will, it needs to be the case that the readiness potential plays a very specific role in the production of our decisions and actions. In particular, the following must be true:

*Possibility 1*    When you make a torn decision, the readiness potential is the cause (or at least *part* of the cause) of how you choose. For instance, when you ordered chocolate ice cream, the readiness potential caused you to choose chocolate over vanilla (or at any rate, it was *part* of the cause of your doing that).

The problem, though, is that there is simply no evidence for the claim that this is what the readiness potential is doing. So my claim here is just this: the readiness potential might be doing something *else*, something that doesn't have anything to do with which option you choose. And to drive this point home, I want to give an example of what it might be doing. There are in fact *many* things that the readiness potential could be doing; I will just describe *one* of these possibilities.

The possibility I will describe is related to what in chapter 5 I called the *third confusion*. The third confusion had to do with the fact that only a certain *feature* of our torn decisions needs to be undetermined. In particular, it needs to be that when we make our torn decisions, *which tied-for-best-option is chosen* is not predetermined by prior events. But everything *else* about the decision can be completely caused by prior events. And what we're going to see now is that the readiness potential could be part of the cause of these *other* features of our torn decisions. Here is one such possibility for what the readiness potential might be doing:

*Possibility 2*    It could be that the readiness potential is part of the cause of the *occurrence* of a decision.

Think again of your decision to order chocolate ice cream. For all we know right now, it could be that both of the following claims are true: (i) the fact that you made a torn decision between chocolate and vanilla was completely caused by prior events; and (ii) the fact that you chose chocolate over vanilla wasn't caused by anything. But given this, it could be that the readiness potential was part of the causal process mentioned in (i). In other words, it could be that the readiness potential was part of the physical brain process that led to you making a torn decision between chocolate and vanilla. And it could be that the readiness potential didn't have anything at all to do with the fact that you chose chocolate over vanilla. And so even if the readiness potential appeared *before* you made your conscious decision, it simply doesn't follow that your choice was predetermined.

So this gives us an alternative story about what the readiness potential might be doing in our torn decisions, aside from causing us to choose specific options. Now, as of right now, there is no good reason to think that this alternative story—Possibility 2—is *true*. But the important point for us is that there's no good reason to think it's *false* either. There's no *evidence* that it's false. In short, the point is that there's no good scientific reason for favoring Possibility 1 over Possibility 2. And that's enough to undermine the argument for the claim that Libet's results disprove free will. The bottom line is this: we don't have any good reason to think that when you make a torn decision, the readiness potential causes you to choose a specific option, and so the presence of the readiness potential doesn't give us any reason to think that your torn decisions aren't the products of your free will.

## The Haynes Studies

All that remains is to evaluate the anti-free-will argument based on the studies of J. D. Haynes. This might seem like the hardest of the anti-free-will arguments to respond to. For, intuitively, Haynes's studies *seem* to deliver a knockout punch to the idea that we have free will.

In fact, Haynes's studies seem to be tailor-made to provide the enemies of free will with a way of responding to what I just said about Libet's studies. My central objection to Libet's argument was that his studies fail to distinguish between the *occurrence* of a torn decision and the issue of *which tied-for-best option is chosen*. More specifically, my objection to the Libet argument is that, for all we know, the readiness potential could be part of what causes our torn decisions to occur without doing anything to cause a specific tied-for-best option to be chosen. But Haynes's studies seem tailor-made to block this sort of response.

Let's recall how the central Haynes study went. Haynes gave his subjects two buttons, one for the left hand and one for the right hand, and he told them to make a decision at some point as to which button to push and to then press the given button as soon as they made their decision. Haynes found that there was unconscious neural activity in two different regions of the brain that predicted whether subjects were about to press the left button or the right button. Moreover, he found that this activity arose as long as seven to ten seconds before the person made a conscious decision to push the given button. These results seem to provide a devastating argument against free will. One might put the argument like this:

If you're about to choose whether to press the left button or the right button, and if somebody watching your brain could predict which button you're going to push a full seven to ten seconds before you make your conscious choice, then clearly, your conscious choice isn't responsible for determining what you do. What you were going to do was already determined before you made your conscious decision. And given this, it doesn't make any sense at all to say that you chose of your own free will. In short, when we make our conscious decisions, if what we're going to do is already settled several seconds *before* we make these decisions, then we simply don't have free will.

This is how the argument is usually presented by people who don't believe in free will. And when the argument is presented like this, it seems extremely powerful. But when you go and look at the journal article in which Haynes's results are published, all sorts of problems start to emerge. As they say, the devil is in the details. And what I want to do now is explain how some of the details of this study completely undermine the argument against free will.

There are two details of this study that I want to discuss. The first has to do with the specific *regions* of the brain in which the pre-conscious-choice neural activity was found; in particular, it was found in the *parietal cortex* (for short, the PC) and in what's known as the *Brodmann area 10* (for short, the BA10). Why this is important will become clear below. The second important detail is this: the pre-choice brain activity that Haynes found (in the PC and BA10 regions) was actually not very good at predicting the outcomes of his subjects' choices. Indeed, it was only 10 percent more accurate than *blind guessing*. If you blindly guess whether subjects will push the left button or the right button, you will be right about 50 percent of the time. And by looking at the PC and BA10 regions of the subjects' brains and using *this* to predict whether they'll push the left button or the right button, you'll be right *at best* 60 percent of the time. This is definitely statistically significant, so it shows *something*. But it's a far cry from 100 percent accuracy. And as I will explain in what follows, this completely undermines the Haynes argument against free will. In short, although Haynes's results definitely show *something*, they *don't* show that we don't have free will.

But let me slow down and explain the significance of the fact that the pre-choice brain activity was found in the PC and BA10 regions of the brain. The strange thing about this is that these regions of the brain are not ordinarily associated with free decisions. Rather, they're associated with *plans, or intentions*. In particular, the PC is associated with the *generation* of plans, and the BA10 is associated with the *storage* of plans. Suppose, for example, that I form a plan to visit Hawaii next summer. Once I've made this plan, I can *remember* it. That means that the plan is stored somewhere in my brain. And there is significant evidence that plans like this are stored in the BA10 region of the brain. And there is also evidence that plans are *generated* in the PC region.

This is really important. In fact, when we combine this with the fact that the neural activity in the PC and the BA10 regions is only 10 percent more predictive than blind guessing, the argument against free will completely falls apart. The reason is that when we put these two facts together, they suggest an interpretation of Haynes's results that's perfectly consistent with free will. In a moment, I'll tell you what this interpretation is. But first, I want to make a background point.

When someone asks you *not* to think about something, it suddenly becomes very difficult to obey them. For instance, if I don't want you to think about Abraham Lincoln right now, one of the worst things I could do is *tell* you not to think about him. If I just say nothing, then the odds that you would think of Lincoln in the next few minutes are vanishingly small. But as soon as I say, "Don't think about Abe Lincoln," it becomes very hard for you to avoid thinking about him, even if you sincerely want to obey me. The problem is that the temptation to think about what you're not supposed to think about can be almost overwhelming.

The same goes for silly little *decisions*, like picking a number between 1 and 10. Suppose I say this to you: "In a minute, I'm going to ask you to pick a number between 1 and 10, *but don't do it yet.*" It's actually very difficult to refrain from thinking of a number in situations like this. Indeed, it's likely that before I can even spit out the second half of my sentence, you will already have thought of a number between 1 and 10. As soon as I tell you that you're going to be asked to pick a number between 1 and 10, you might pick the number 7 before you even hear me say that you shouldn't choose yet.

Now, once you hear me tell you that you're not supposed to pick yet, you might try to undo what you already did. In other words, you might try to *un*pick the number 7. But notice that the result of this will probably not be that 7 gets "put back into the hopper." Instead, it will be that 7 is eliminated from contention all together. This is because we can't turn ourselves into random number generators. The problem is that you won't be able to forget that you already thought of the number 7. So after a minute passes and I tell you to go ahead and pick a number, it's extremely unlikely that you'll pick 7 again. If you did, you wouldn't think that you were being truly random and that it was just a coincidence that you picked 7 twice in a row; you'd think you were being a *moron*, always responding in the same way to the request to think of a number. And you'd probably also think you were *cheating*—that you were flagrantly disobeying the command not to choose in advance. So even if you didn't realize this, I think the real result of undoing your choice would very likely be that 7 would simply be eliminated from contention.

But now suppose that instead of telling you that you're going to have to pick a number between 1 and 10, I told you that you're going to have to pick a number between 1 and 2. And suppose that you instantly thought of the number 2. Now, what's going to happen when I tell you that I don't want you to choose yet, that I want you to wait sixty seconds and *then* pick a number. You're liable to think something like this to yourself:

> Oh, crap, I already thought of 2. Well, I'll just *un*pick it. Yeah, that's the ticket—that's *easy*. OK, it's unpicked. I'm not thinking anything now.

*Makes so much Sense!*

But now, if the result of this is that 2 is eliminated from consideration, then the only option left is 1. So unless you really manage to completely forget about the fact that you chose the number 2 before, the choice you end up making is not going to be truly random. It's going to be weirdly influenced by your attempt to follow the instructions despite the fact that you started off by picking the number 2.

So that's *one* point. Here's another point: even if you don't start out by thinking of one of the two numbers, it's actually very difficult to *keep* yourself from thinking of one of them. Try it right now. Flip an hourglass over and tell yourself that you're not going to think of 1 or 2 until all the sand runs out and that, when the sand *does* run out, you're going to choose one of the two numbers. It's actually very difficult not to think of one of the two numbers. I'm not saying that you *can't* succeed in this task. Of course you can. For instance, you might manage to somehow distract yourself and think about something else entirely. But you might not succeed. In short, the point here is that *sometimes*, when we're asked not to think about something, we *fail*. This might make human beings sound kind of lame, but we all know it's true.

Now, here's the really important point for us. You might fail in this task *even if you don't realize it*. You might subconsciously think of the number 1, and you might subconsciously store the plan to pick that number when the time comes. This point shouldn't be controversial at all. Here are two things that we *know* to be true about human beings: first, it's very difficult to avoid thinking about something when someone tells you not to think about it; and second, we do all sorts of things unconsciously. We don't do *everything* unconsciously, but it's clear that we do a *lot* of things unconsciously. When we put these two points together, we get the following (highly probable) hypothesis:

> If you take a group of human subjects and you tell them that in sixty seconds they're going to be asked to pick the number 1 or the number 2, and if you tell them not to pick yet—in other words, if you tell them to wait until the sixty seconds are up before they choose—at least *some* of these subjects will (without realizing it) fail to wait the full sixty seconds before choosing. In other words, at least some of the people will subconsciously think of one of the two numbers and subconsciously store the plan to pick that number when the time comes.

Again, given what we know about ourselves, this seems extremely plausible. In fact, it seems almost *obvious*. I would be really surprised if it *wasn't* true.

This is all just background. But it's highly relevant to the Haynes studies. In fact, it seems to give us an interpretation of the Haynes results that's perfectly consistent with the existence of free will. So without any further ado, let me give you the interpretation:

*An interpretation of the results of the Haynes study that's perfectly consistent with the existence of free will* A significant percentage of the subjects in Haynes's study (say, 20 percent of them) unconsciously failed to make truly spontaneous decisions about whether to press the right button or the left button. They genuinely *wanted* to follow Haynes's instructions, but for whatever reason, and without realizing it, they unconsciously formed prior-to-choice plans to push one of the two buttons. They unconsciously stored this information in their brains, and then when the time came, these plans were activated. In other words, the regions of the brain where these plans were stored were activated. And this brain activity caused the subjects to choose in the predetermined ways in which they had unconsciously planned on choosing. This explains why (in *some* subjects) there was prior-to-choice brain activity in the PC and BA10 regions of the brain (and, remember, these regions are associated with the formation and storage of *plans*, not free decisions). It also explains why this brain activity predicts whether subjects will choose to push the left button or the right button. And finally, it also explains why using this brain activity to predict how subjects will choose is only 10 percent better than blind guessing—the reason is that *not all* subjects unconsciously failed to make spontaneous decisions. Only *some* subjects formed unconscious plans about what they were going to do. *Most* subjects managed to avoid doing this. Most of them managed to make truly spontaneous decisions. (Of course, the claim here isn't that most of us have free will, but some of us don't. The claim is that *all* of us *sometimes* fail to be free. We are all *sometimes* driven by things like unconscious plans. But we aren't *always* driven by such things.)

The first point to note here is that if this is the right interpretation of Haynes's results, then there is no problem here for free will. All these results show is that sometimes our decisions are influenced by unconscious factors. But we already *knew* this. And as I've already pointed out, it doesn't follow from this that we don't have free will. To establish that we don't have free will, you would have to argue that *all* of our torn decisions are predetermined by unconscious factors. But the Haynes studies don't give us any good reason to think that that's true. And so they don't give us any good reason to deny the existence of free will.

In a moment, I'll say a bit more to justify the claim that Haynes's results don't give us any good reason to doubt the

The claim is that *all* of us *sometimes* fail to be free. We are all *sometimes* driven by things like unconscious plans. But we aren't *always* driven by such things.

existence of free will. But first, I want to say a little bit about the style of argument that I've used here to respond to Libet and Haynes. Whenever we perform a scientific study, we have to *interpret* the data before we can draw any conclusions. What this means is that in order to arrive at the conclusion that we don't have free will, we have to interpret the Libet–Haynes data in a certain, specific way. Therefore, one way to respond to the Libet–Haynes argument is to offer an *alternative interpretation* in which their conclusion doesn't follow. In other words, we can block their argument by telling a story that explains *why* they got the data they did *without* admitting that we don't have free will.

Now, whenever you respond to a scientific argument in this way, you have to make sure that the alternative interpretation you're giving isn't a *cockamamie* story. Let me give you an example of what I mean by this. We have a mountain of evidence linking smoking to lung cancer. Now, strictly speaking, all this shows is that there is a *statistical correlation* between smoking and lung cancer. We have to *infer* from this that smoking can *cause* lung cancer. Therefore, if you wanted to, you could try to respond to the argument for the claim that smoking can cause lung cancer by providing an alternative interpretation of the data. For instance, one might say something like this:

> *Alternative interpretation of the statistical correlation between smoking and lung cancer*　Sure, there's a

statistical correlation between smoking and lung cancer, but this doesn't mean that smoking *causes* lung cancer. There might be some other explanation of the statistical correlation. For instance, it could be that there's some hidden gene that we don't know about that independently causes two different things, namely, the desire to smoke and lung cancer. If this is right, then there would definitely be a statistical correlation between smoking and lung cancer. But smoking wouldn't cause lung cancer. Therefore, since for all we know right now, this is *possible*, we can't conclude that smoking causes lung cancer. And so if you want to smoke, there's no good reason to resist the temptation.

Well, it's certainly *possible* that this alternative story is true. But what are the *odds* of this? It just seems extremely unlikely. In short, the story that's being told here is a *cockamamie* story.

There's a general lesson to be learned here. If you want to respond to a scientific argument, you can't do it by providing a cockamamie story to explain the data. You have to do it by providing an alternative story (or an alternative interpretation of the data) that's *just as plausible*—or just as likely to be true—as the original interpretation of the data.

So in our case, we have to ask whether the alternative interpretation of the data that I'm suggesting here is just as plausible, or just as *probable*, as the interpretations that are offered by people like Libet and Haynes. The answer is that it is.

In the case of Libet's studies, this is entirely obvious. As I pointed out above, we don't have any idea what the function of the readiness potential is. The enemies of free will just *assume* that the readiness potential causes a specific option to be chosen. But it's *just as likely* that the readiness potential is relevant only to the *occurrences* of our torn decisions and not to the issue of which tied-for-best option is chosen. So my interpretation of the data is no less likely to be true than Libet's interpretation.

In the case of Haynes's data, I want to make an even stronger claim. I want to argue that my interpretation is *more* plausible—or more likely to be true—than the interpretation that's hostile to free will. This other interpretation says that the prior-to-conscious-choice brain activity in the PC and BA10 regions is an early neural signature of the brain already making the decision. Call this the *anti-free-will interpretation*. There are at least three different arguments for thinking that my interpretation of Haynes's data is more plausible than this anti-free-will interpretation. Here are the three arguments:

1. We have strong independent evidence for the hypothesis that the PC and BA10 regions of the brain are relevant not to free decisions but to the

formation and storage of plans and intentions. Therefore, since my interpretation takes the brain activity in those regions to be related to the storage of long-term plans, it fits with what we already know about those regions, and so it is more plausible than the anti-free-will interpretation, which takes this activity to be an early neural signature of the decision itself.

2. The fact that there is a *seven-to-ten-second time gap* between the brain activity in the PC and BA10 regions and the conscious decision actually counts as strong evidence that that activity is *not* part of the decision. This is a bit ironic because, intuitively, the seven-to-ten-second gap is the thing that makes Haynes's results so *striking*. When you first hear about these studies, you're likely to think something like this:

> *Holy crap!* If neuroscientists can predict how I'll choose seven to ten seconds before I make a conscious decision, then how on Earth could I have free will?

But on further reflection, the seven-to-ten-second time gap turns out to be part of what undoes the Haynes argument. This is because we have really strong reasons to think that human beings are way faster than this when it comes to making decisions. There is significant experimental evidence that shows that we can make decisions in *less than half a second*. And what's more, we all *know* that this is true. We have all had lots of experience making snap decisions in way less than seven seconds. Therefore, since we know that decisions take less than seven seconds, it's not plausible that the brain activity that Haynes observed—a full seven to ten seconds before the conscious choice—was an early neural signature of the conscious choice. It's much more plausible to suppose that the brain activity in the PC and BA10 regions is doing something else. And my interpretation provides a compelling story about what this brain activity is doing—it's related to the storage of a long-term plan that was made unconsciously and unwittingly by the subject.

3. My interpretation explains why using the brain activity in the PC and BA10 regions is only 10 percent more accurate than blind guessing. It's because only *some* of the subjects unwittingly formed unconscious plans about what they were going to do. Some of them didn't do this. Some of them managed to refrain from doing this so that their decisions were genuinely spontaneous, last-second choices. On the other hand, the anti-free-will interpretation of

Haynes's results *doesn't* explain why using the brain activity in the PC and BA10 regions is only 10 percent more accurate than blind guessing. People who favor this anti-free-will interpretation have no option but to say that the reason there's only a 10 percent increase in accuracy here is that we're just not good enough yet at gathering data from people's brains. This seems like a real stretch to me.

So, again, it seems to me that my interpretation of the data is much better than the anti-free-will interpretation. Now, I don't want to claim that I have *proven* that my interpretation is definitely the right one. It is, of course, possible that the brain activity in the PC and BA10 regions *is* an early neural signature of the decision. But there's no evidence for this. In short, there's no good reason to think that the anti-free-will interpretation is the right interpretation. And this means that the Haynes study just doesn't give us any good reason to doubt the existence of free will.

### Ditto for Advocates of the Spiritual, Religious View—Sort Of

In chapter 6, I responded to the random-or-predetermined argument against free will. While I was responding to that argument, I more or less assumed that the materialistic, scientific view of humans is correct; in other words, I assumed that human beings do not have nonphysical souls. But at the end of the chapter, I pointed out that people who endorse the spiritual, religious view of humans—people who think that we *do* have nonphysical souls—can respond to the random-or-predetermined argument in essentially the same way that I did.

I want to make a similar point here. But as we'll see, in this case, there's a bit of a catch. In this chapter, I have responded to the scientific argument against free will, and once again, in constructing my response, I have more or less assumed that the materialistic, scientific view of humans is correct. But if you endorse the spiritual, religious view of humans, you can respond in a very similar way:

1. You can respond to the psychological arguments by admitting that our torn decisions are *sometimes* influenced by unconscious factors that are out of our control, and you can maintain that there is no evidence that our torn decisions are *always* caused by unconscious factors.

2. You can respond to the Libet study by pointing out (as I did above) that there is no good evidence for the claim that when we make our torn decisions, the readiness potential is part of a physical process that causes us to choose in the specific ways that we do.

3. You can respond to the Haynes study by pointing out that the pre-choice neural activity in the PC and BA10 regions of the brain is most likely a sign of the fact that some small percentage of the subjects (say, 20 percent of them) unwittingly and unconsciously form pre-choice long-term plans to push either the left button or the right button.

So if you endorse the spiritual, religious view, you can respond to the scientific argument against free will in essentially the same way that I have responded to it on behalf of those who endorse the materialistic, scientific view of humans.

But like I said before, I think there's a catch here. The scientific arguments don't give us any reason to doubt the existence of free will, but it seems to me that they do give us some reason to worry about the spiritual, religious view itself. In other words, the studies I've been discussing (and other studies like them) seem to give us some initial reason to think that we just don't have nonphysical souls. I am not going to try to provide a complete argument for this here, but I'd like to say just a few words about it.

One point here is that it's hard to see why a nonphysical soul would have subconscious mental states. But let me ignore this and focus on Haynes's results. If we have nonphysical souls, then why should we have to store our plans in the BA10 region of the brain? Why can't we just store them nonphysically in our souls? This is, of course, just a special case of a much more general problem. If we have nonphysical souls, then why would we need to have brains to carry off our mental actions? Or to put the point the other way around, if all mental states and events correspond to neural states and events, then why should we believe in nonphysical souls at all? It seems that all mental states and events have locations in the brain. Beliefs are stored in this region; plans are stored in that region; decisions occur here; inferences occur there. Why do we need to posit a soul at all? It seems that the brain can do it all by itself. In fact, given that there's a neural signature of everything that happens in the human mind, it seems that the brain does do it all by itself.

But, again, I'm not trying to argue here that we don't have nonphysical souls. I'm just throwing this out there as food for thought.

# CONCLUSION

If what I've argued in this book is right, then the anti-free-will arguments that have been put forward recently by philosophers, psychologists, and neuroscientists simply don't work. And so we don't have any good reason to doubt the existence of free will.

But a word of warning is in order. I have not argued in this book that we *do* have free will. I've simply blocked the arguments for the claim that we *don't* have free will. Now, you might think that since, intuitively, it *seems* to us that we have free will, the burden of proof is on the enemies of free will. So you might think that since we have found that their arguments don't work, it is rational for us to believe that we *do* have free will.

I think this would be a mistake. We haven't just found in this book that the anti-free-will arguments don't work. We've also found that the question of whether we have free will is not something that we can answer by intuition or common sense. On the contrary, the claim that we have free will is a controversial scientific hypothesis about the causation of our torn decisions. In particular, to say that we have free will is to say that the following hypothesis is true:

> At least sometimes, when we make our torn decisions, nothing causes us to choose in the ways that we do.[1]

This is not a commonsense truism. It is a controversial claim of neuroscience. In fact, it seems to me that the question of whether we have free will is so hard that, given our current knowledge of the brain, we are nowhere near ready to answer it. To obtain compelling evidence for the claim that we have free will, we would need to do all of the following:

1. First and foremost, we would need to find our torn decisions in the brain. In other words, we would need to figure out which neural events are our torn decisions. By all accounts, we aren't even close to being able to do this.

2. Second, if we could point at a neural event and say with confidence that it was a torn decision, we would also need to be able to say which feature of that neural event corresponded to the chosen option. In other words, we would need to be able to look at a neural event of the kind I'm talking about and *read off*

In fact, it seems to me that the question of whether we have free will is so hard that, given our current knowledge of the brain, we are nowhere near ready to answer it.

*of it* whether it was a chocolate-over-vanilla decision, or a vanilla-over-chocolate decision, or whatever.

3. Finally, we would need to study these neural events and figure out whether anything causes the given tied-for-best options to be chosen. In particular, we would need to find evidence for the claim that at least sometimes, *nothing* causes them to be chosen.

If we could do all of this, then we would have good scientific evidence for the claim that when we make our torn decisions, at least sometimes, nothing makes us choose in the ways that we do. And this would give us good reason to believe that we have free will.

But right now, we're nowhere near ready to do any of this. And so what we should say here is that as of right now, we don't know whether we have free will. We should say that this is an open scientific question.

That's not so bad. Given that there are people out there telling you that they've already established that we don't have free will, it's not so bad to be left with the conclusion that we don't know whether we have free will.

We have found here that the enemies of free will seriously overstate their case. The truth is that they don't know anywhere near enough about how the human brain works to conclude with any sort of certainty that we don't have free will. As we've seen, the arguments that people have put forward against free will are based on some assumptions that are completely unfounded.

What I'm saying now is that we shouldn't make the same mistake that these people have made. We shouldn't overstate the case *for* free will. We shouldn't make unfounded assumptions. We should be careful and skeptical. We should recognize when we're ignorant and not try to pretend that we aren't. The reality is that (a) the question of free will is a super-hard question about the causation of certain neural events; and (b) we are pretty ignorant on this topic. Neuroscience has made some truly amazing strides in the last few decades. But this science is still in its infancy. We just aren't ready right now to answer the question of free will. And what's more—given what we would need to do to settle this question—it is unlikely that we will be able to answer it during our lives. It is very likely that those of us who are alive right now will all be dead and buried before human beings can answer the question of free will with any kind of authority.

I want to make one more point about being skeptical. You should always beware of someone throwing a bunch of scientific studies at you and telling you that these studies establish X, Y, or Z. You can't trust people on stuff like this. You have to read the journal articles yourself to see what they show. And if you don't have time to do that, you should be skeptical. In short, you should remain unconvinced.

If the same study has been performed numerous times, in many different labs, spread out across many years, and if all of the experts in the given area agree that a certain conclusion follows, then this gives us some reason to think that the conclusion is probably true. But you can't trust an argument that's based on an isolated study, especially when it involves a controversial inference about what the results show. In situations like this, it is always better to remain skeptical and unconvinced.

**Causation**
See the entries for *Deterministic causation* and *Probabilistic causation*.

**Compatibilism**
This is the view that free will is compatible with determinism. Thus, on this view, even if all of your actions and decisions are completely predetermined—even if they're all completely caused by events that took place billions of years ago—it can still make sense to say that you have free will.

**Determinism**
Roughly speaking, this is the view that all events are completely caused by prior events. More precisely, it's the view that a complete statement of the laws of nature, together with a complete description of the universe at some specific time, logically entails a complete description of the universe at all later times.

**Deterministic causation**
To say that an event was deterministically caused by prior events is to say that it was completely caused by prior events. In other words, it's to say that it was completely predetermined, so that prior events forced it to happen in the one and only way that it could have happened.

**Empirical science**
An empirical science is a science like physics, chemistry, biology, psychology, or neuroscience. These sciences are concerned with characterizing the nature of the physical world, and their methodologies are based in observation and experimentation. Empirical sciences can be contrasted with disciplines like mathematics and logic, whose methodologies are usually not empirical—that is, they are usually not based in observation or experimentation.

**Free will**
This term is notoriously difficult to define. Moreover, the question of how it should be defined is extremely controversial. For two very popular definitions,

see the entries for *Hume-style free will* and *Not-predetermined free will*. Many philosophers think that the term "free will" is essentially synonymous with "Hume-style free will"; others think it's synonymous with "not-predetermined free will"; and still others think that some other definition needs to be given. But, again, all of these views are controversial.

### Hume-style free will
Roughly speaking, we can take Hume-style free will to be the ability to *do what you want*. More precisely, we can say that a person has Hume-style free will if and only if he or she is capable of acting in accordance with his or her choices and choosing in accordance with his or her desires.

### Indeterminism
This is just the view that determinism is false. In other words, it's the view that at least some events are not completely predetermined by prior events.

### Materialism
This is a term that gets used to mean many different things. In this book, I use it to refer to the view that human beings are purely physical creatures, or that they're made entirely of *matter* and that they do not have nonphysical souls.

### Neural processes
See the entry for *Neuron*.

### Neuron
A neuron is a nerve cell. The most important thing about neurons is that they're electrically excitable. When an electrical signal travels down a neuron, we say that it *fires*. There are trillions of neurons in the brain, and there's a sense in which they "talk to each other"; when one neuron fires, it can cause other neurons to fire, and in this way, information can be transmitted through the brain. In this book, I often speak of *neural processes*, and when I do that, I'm talking about brain processes that involve the firing of neurons.

### Neuroscience
Neuroscience is an interdisciplinary study of the nervous system. So, of course, neuroscientists study neurons and neural processes.

### Nonrandomness

See the entry for *Randomness*.

### Not-predetermined free will

To say that a person has not-predetermined free will is to say that at least some of his or her decisions have the following two traits: (i) they're not predetermined by prior events, and (ii) they're nonrandom in the sense that the person in question is in control of which option is chosen, so that he or she is the *author* of the choice, or the *source* of the choice. Thus, to simplify this a bit, if we suppose that you just made a conscious decision, then to say that that decision was a product of your free will (in the sense of not-predetermined free will) is to say that (a) *you* did it, and (b) nothing *made* you do it.

### NPD free will

See the entry for *Not-predetermined free will*. "NPD free will" is just an abbreviation for that term.

### Probabilistic causation

To say that an event was probabilistically caused by prior events is to say that it was caused by prior events but that these prior events didn't force it to happen. Rather, the prior events simply increased the probability that the event in question would happen.

### Randomness

This is a term that gets used in many different ways. The uses of the term in this book have to do with the question of whether our decisions occur randomly or nonrandomly. To say that a decision occurred randomly can mean many different things, but the two most important meanings for the purposes of this book are as follows. First, by saying that a decision occurred randomly, you might mean to say that it was completely uncaused. And second, you might mean to say that the person in question wasn't in control of the decision, or wasn't the author of the decision, or wasn't the real source of the decision. Thus, if we're using the term in this second way, then to say that a decision of mine occurred *non*randomly is to say that I was in control of the decision; in particular, it's to say that I was in control of which option was chosen; or to put the point a different way, it's to say that I was the source of the decision, or the author of the decision. An important question is whether a decision can be nonrandom in this sense while simultaneously being random in the sense of being completely uncaused. I argue in this book (in chapter 6) that this *is* possible.

**Torn decisions**

A torn decision is a conscious decision in which you have multiple options and you're torn as to which option is best. More precisely, you have multiple options that seem to you to be more or less tied for best, so that you feel completely unsure—or entirely torn—as to what you ought to do. And you decide while feeling torn.

# NOTES

**Chapter 4**

1. Of course, when I say that we have Hume-style free will, I don't mean to suggest that we can do everything we want to do. I want to jump off the Empire State Building, glide around in circles over New York City, and then land softly in Central Park; but, of course, I can't do this. But I still have Hume-style free will, because I can do a lot of what I want to do. Now, some people have less Hume-style free will than most of us do. For instance, whereas I can walk down the street and go to the movies, people who are in jail can't do this, even if they want to. But these people still have some Hume-style free will. For instance, if some inmate has a book sitting next to his bed, and if he wants to pick it up and start reading, then (in most situations) he can do this.

2. The William James quote comes from his paper "The Dilemma of Determinism" (on page 149 in the version of the paper listed in the bibliography). And the Kant quotes come from his book *The Critique of Practical Reason* (on pages 95–96 in the version of the book listed in the bibliography).

**Chapter 6**

1. This is a slight simplification. Strictly speaking, what we should say here is that (i) if our torn decisions are *deterministically* caused by prior events, then we *don't* have free will; and (ii) if our torn decisions are completely *un*caused, then we *do* have free will; and (iii) if our torn decisions are probabilistically (but not deterministically) caused, then we have *partial* free will.

**Chapter 8**

1. This is a slight simplification. A torn decision could be *probabilistically* caused without being deterministically caused, and in this scenario, it could still be *partially* free.

# FURTHER READINGS

For an introductory-level discussion of the philosophical problem of free will, see:

Campbell, Joseph Keim. *Free Will*. Cambridge: Polity Press, 2011.

Kane, Robert. *A Contemporary Introduction to Free Will*. Oxford: Oxford University Press, 2005.

O'Connor, Timothy. "Free Will." In *Stanford Encyclopedia of Philosophy*, 2010, http://plato.stanford.edu/entries/freewill/.

Pink, Thomas. *Free Will: A Very Short Introduction*. Oxford: Oxford University Press, 2004.

For an introductory-level attack on free will, see:

Harris, Sam. *Free Will*. New York: Free Press, 2012.

For more academic attacks on free will, see:

Pereboom, Derk. *Living without Free Will*. Cambridge: Cambridge University Press, 2001.

Wegner, Daniel M. *The Illusion of Conscious Will*. Cambridge, MA: MIT Press, 2002.

For an academic defense of free will, see:

Balaguer, Mark. *Free Will as an Open Scientific Problem*. Cambridge, MA: MIT Press, 2010.

# BIBLIOGRAPHY

Harris, Sam. *Free Will*. New York: Free Press, 2012.

Haynes, John-Dylan. "Decoding and Predicting Intentions." *Annals of the New York Academy of Sciences* 1224 (2011): 9–21.

Hume, David. *An Inquiry Concerning Human Understanding*. Indianapolis, IN: Bobbs-Merrill, 1955 (originally published 1748).

James, William. "The Dilemma of Determinism." In *The Will to Believe: Human Immortality*, 145–183. New York: Dover, 1956 (essay originally published 1884).

Kant, Immanuel. *The Critique of Practical Reason*. Trans. T. K. Abbott. New York: Longman, Green, 1927 (originally published 1788).

Libet, Benjamin, and Associates. "Time of Conscious Intention to Act in Relation to Cerebral Potential." *Brain* 106 (3) (1983): 623–642.

Wegner, Daniel M. *The Illusion of Conscious Will*. Cambridge, MA: MIT Press, 2002.

# INDEX

**MARK BALAGUER** is Professor in the Department of Philosophy at California State University, Los Angeles. He is the author of *Platonism and Anti-Platonism in Mathematics* and *Free Will as an Open Scientific Question* (MIT Press).